KEN GOODMAN

Phonics Phacts

HEINEMANN
Portsmouth, NH

Heinemann
A division of Reed Publishing (USA) Inc.
361 Hanover Street, Portsmouth, NH 03801-3912
Offices and agents throughout the world

Published simultaneously by Heinemann in the United States
and Scholastic Canada Ltd. in Canada. All rights reserved.
First printing 1993

ISBN 0-435-08810-6 (Heinemann)

Cover design by Yüksel Hassan

Library of Congress Cataloging-in-Publication Data

Goodman, Kenneth S.
[Phonics phacts]
Ken Goodman's Phonics Phacts / Kenneth S. Goodman.
p. cm.
Includes bibliographical references.
ISBN 0-435-08810-6
1. Reading (Elementary) — Phonetic method. I. Title. II. Title:
Phonics phacts. III. Title: Phonics facts.
LB1573.3.G66 1993
372.4'145—dc20   93-32338
                                  CIP

Printed in Canada by Best Gagné Book Manufacturers
93 94 95 96 97   9 8 7 6 5 4 3 2 1

Over 50% recycled paper
including 10% post
consumer fibre
Plus de 50 p. 100 de
papier recyclé dont 10 p.
100 de fibres post-
consommation.

M - Official mark of Environment Canada
M - Marque officielle d'Environnement Canada.

*This book is dedicated to
the pursuit of truth
and to
the liberation of teachers and learners
from the shackles
of imposed ignorance.*

Acknowledgements

Too many people have contributed to the knowledge and experience I drew on in writing this book for me to hope to acknowledge every debt.

First, there are the children, especially all those who read for me as part of my miscue research. They were the reality I tested my ideas and understandings against. But they were also a constant reminder to me of *why* I was doing research and writing. It has always been on their behalf that I've sought to understand literacy, literacy development and literacy instruction.

Then I must acknowledge uncounted teachers from many parts of the world, teachers I've observed and teachers who have talked and collaborated with me in many ways. Their classrooms were another aspect of the reality my understandings had to serve. And here, at least, I can acknowledge a special few, those who have been closest to my work. In particular I thank my own daughters — two present teachers, Debra Goodman and Wendy Hood, and one former teacher, Karen Goodman — and the teachers who became my doctoral students.

I also need to acknowledge two other special groups of teachers: those at Borton primary magnet school in Tucson who are my colleagues in an undergraduate whole language block program at the University of Arizona, and those who are members of the Tucson TAWL group. I must include, too, all the teachers who have opened their classrooms to me, who have shared personal vignettes and examples, who have raised tough questions, who have taken my ideas and turned them into reality. All these teachers have contributed, directly or indirectly, to this book.

Next, I want to acknowledge the community of professional teacher educators, researchers and writers with whom I communicate, at my own university, in professional associations, and through journals, e-mail networks and other forms of correspondence. Professional organizations like the NCTE and IRA have provided me with forums for presenting and discussing my ideas. Particularly, I must acknowledge my support group, the Center for Expansion of Language and Thinking. CELT members have listened critically and patiently, and have shared their own insights unselfishly.

Adrian Peetoom, as editor of both this book and *What's Whole in Whole Language?*, has helped me immeasurably and made sure that I reach my intended audience. Thanks also to Peter Fries and David Freeman, linguists who read the manuscript and saved me some embarrassments.

And finally I must acknowledge my partner, friend, colleague, collaborator, co-researcher and wife, Yetta Goodman. She's been at the same time my most encouraging and most critical reader. Thanks Yetta, thanks Adrian. Thanks to you all.

Contents

1

*The role
of phonics in
reading is perhaps
the most misunderstood
aspect of language
education
today.*

Heat without light

The role of phonics in reading, in learning to read and in reading instruction is probably the most widely misunderstood and misrepresented aspect of language education today. In fact, the word itself has become so politically charged that it's difficult to discuss it rationally with anyone. Here is a good example:

> "For too long, we have been unwilling to deal with the root cause of the problem of illiteracy in America: the flawed methods we have used to teach our children to read. Research shows phonics is the most effective way to teach people to read. It's the way most of us learned to read. But it fell out of use in the last 20 years, with disastrous consequences." (Armstrong, 1989, p. 1)

This definitive statement comes not from an educator or a researcher but from Senator William Armstrong of Colorado speaking on the floor of the United States Senate. "Phonics" has become more than a technical term in the study or teaching of written language; it's become a political buzzword, a cause. The Senate Republican Policy Committee white paper on literacy ends with a series of school "examples." Under each, the slogan TEACH INTENSIVE SYSTEMATIC PHONICS is printed.

Phonics is a stick to beat the teaching profession with, sometimes with faint praise. The following quote is from an Andrew Nikiforuk column in Canada's leading newspaper, *The Globe and Mail*. Nikiforuk refers to the work of Dr. Carl Kline, emeritus professor of child psychology:

"... the majority of struggling readers, he contends, are the products of whole-language reading approaches that have neglected to include the structured and sequential teaching of multi-sensory phonics. . . . 'I'm not criticizing teachers,' adds Dr. Kline quickly. 'Most want to do well. But they have not been trained well by faculties of education.'" (December 11, 1992)

Here is Blumenfeld's more strident voice:

"Never have American professors and teachers acted more irresponsibly in the face of a serious national problem of growing illiteracy. If it were in our power to do so, we'd fire the whole lot of them tomorrow." (Blumenfeld, 1989, p. 5)

The "cause" even attracts some professional educators, who judge every new understanding of the reading process and every change in reading instruction by whether it's for or against phonics instruction. Richard Anderson makes the following statement:

"Educational research in the United States has consistently shown that children make more progress in reading, on the average, when they receive systematic phonics instruction in the early grades. Why, then, were programs known for strong phonics recommended for rejection (by the CA textbook selection commission) . . .

"My hunch is that the main reason is the changing winds of ideological fashion. Something called the 'whole language movement' has an enthusiastic following in California reading circles . . . the most zealous proponents of 'whole language' are as noteworthy for what they are against as what they are for. They absolutely proscribe 'teaching skills in isolation,' which in their minds rules out traditional, systematic approaches to phonics." (Quoted in Hinds, undated, p. 14)

The politics of phonics has made it difficult for the education profession and the public in general to learn much about what phonics really is. Politicians often reduce complex issues to suspicious simplicity to make voters feel confident that solutions are within easy grasp. But we all know how seldom simplistic promises, so glibly offered when elections loom, translate into longterm benefits. We also know that easily offered slogans can stand in the way of genuine efforts to discover the real roots of complex problems.

My intention in writing this book is not to attack the "phonics-phirst pholks" (or is it the "fonics-first folks"?), but simply to help teachers and parents understand better the whole topic of phonics so they feel more comfortable evaluating the conflicting views they are presented with. To do that I'll define phonics and then address three topics: the science, teaching and politics of phonics.

Preliminary observations

Because I've spent many years studying the reading process, I've come to understand what phonics is and how it works in English. For my research, I asked a large number of people of a wide range of language backgrounds and reading proficiencies to read whole texts aloud while I carefully noted down what they said. Then I analyzed the differences between what they actually said and what I expected them to say on the basis of the text. I called those differences "miscues," to avoid the more negative "errors."

My premise is that nothing people do when they read is random or accidental. On the contrary, everything readers do as they respond to a printed text results from their attempt to make sense of it.

But just how do people go about making sense of text? I asked myself. Simply speaking, what I found was that readers use three types of information to construct meaning from printed text:

➤ *visual information* from the print;

➤ *sound information* from their oral language;

➤ *phonic information* from their understanding of how written and oral language relate.

Two more types of knowledge are important in making sense of a printed text:

➤ their knowledge of the language's *grammatical structure*;

➤ their knowledge that *coherent meaning* can be constructed from an authentic literacy event.

There's no doubt about it: reading is a complex process!

In my research and in building my theory, I drew on the work of linguists, psycholinguists and sociolinguists. I came to understand the science of how sounds and letters work together in an alphabetic language, and in this book I'll demonstrate my conclusion that *phonic relationships are between the patterns and systems of oral and written language, not between individual letters and sounds.*

To do so, I'll try to present a straightforward explanation of what phonics is, how it works in reading and writing, and how readers use various types of information: graphophonic (some years ago I coined that word to refer to the combination of phonological, orthographic and phonic information), morphological, syntactic, semantic and pragmatic. I'll offer explicit evidence from real language and authentic language use, avoiding technical language as much as I can and still keep my explanations scientific. Too much writing about phonics is too simplistic.

Another problem, especially within the teaching profession, is that many authors writing about phonics are concerned more with *teaching* than with *language,* more with *methods* than with accurate phonics *facts*, more with *teaching about* phonics than with *using* phonics. Teachers are often required to teach phonics with little personal knowledge of it, and sometimes with a good deal of misinformation about it. (I once heard the great linguist, Charles Fries, call such misinformation "linguistic science-fiction.") The more central the role assigned to instruction about phonics as part of reading instruction, the more important it is that the information teachers have about phonics be scientific and accurate.

A personal statement

I'm well aware that this book may not be readily accepted by everyone. Especially in the United States, but also in Canada, Australia, New Zealand and England, there are people who will reject it as an attempt on my part to grind my own ax.

It's true that it is an intensely personal book. It puts phonics into the context of my own understanding of how the reading process works, how reading is learned and how teaching best supports that learning. But it's based solidly not only on my own many years of research, but also on the work of other researchers. And while it represents my own view, that view is one that a widening circle of teachers and researchers hold and that forms the basis for much of the innovative practice in whole language reading instruction.

Here is what I intend and hope to do:

➤ tackle misconceptions about and misrepresentations of phonics, particularly English phonics;

➤ show how these misunderstandings conflict with scientific realities;

➤ question how good the information about phonics is in so-called phonics programs, and how valid it is to teach reading through instruction about phonics;

➤ suggest some of the reasons why misconceptions about phonics persist and why it has taken so long for segments of the research, teaching and general communities to accept easily confirmed scientific concepts.

This book, then, is my personal statement of scientific belief about an important topic. To teachers and parents, I offer it as a source of accurate information about important aspects of language and language learning. To those who say "but it's just your opinion," I offer it as invitation to suggest better alternative explanations for the evidence I cite. To those who get caught in political crossfires, I offer it as a source of information to counter misinformation.

2

*English
may be more
complex than most, but
no language corresponds
on a pure one-to-one
letter-to-sound
basis.*

Some basic misconceptions

This chapter provides some definitions for commonly used terms, describes various writing systems, and draws broad connections between oral and written language.

Defining phonics

The simple definitions some people use for phonics, like "letter-sound relationships" or "phoneme-grapheme relationships," aren't accurate or sufficient. Phonics is much more complex than a set of one-letter-to-one-sound correspondences. The term needs to be carefully distinguished from other linguistic terms that are sometimes used as synonyms.

Phonology

Phonology is the general term linguists use to refer to the *system of sounds an oral language uses*. Each language chooses a range of sounds that differs, to some extent, from the range of sounds chosen by other languages. (The term also refers to the study of the sound system of a language.)

Phonetics

Phonetics deals more specifically with the *characteristics of speech sounds*. For instance, "acoustic phonetics" looks at the qualities a speech sound has, the distinctive features that a human ear or an acoustic instrument is able to detect. "Articulatory phonetics" classifies the distinctive features of speech sounds

5

according to what parts of the mouth and throat are used to produce them: labials employ lips, dentals employ teeth, etc. In both, phoneticians look for distinctive features.

Phonemes

Phonemes are the *significant symbols perceived by speakers of a particular oral language*. Each language uses only some of all possible language sounds, of course, and only some of the particular features of those sounds that make them different. Every phoneme of a language includes a range of similar sounds in different sound sequences that users of that language *perceive* as the same. What's important to understand is that perception happens in the brain, not in the ears, and the brain can treat sounds as the same when they are quite different, and as different when they are identical except for one tiny variation. Studies show that listeners sometimes perceive the same sound as different depending on the sounds that precede or follow it, for instance. So, to say it another way, *phonemes are collections of sounds treated as a single perceptual unit by the listener*.

In English, for example, there is a group of consonant phonemes that have a common feature: they are all what we call "stops." But they differ in other features. The following chart shows the differences we find in most contexts and most dialects.

Note: Throughout this book I'll use the linguist's convention of putting phonemes between / / and letters between < >.

STOPS	Bilabials (lips together)	Alveolar (tip of tongue to upper gums)	Velar (tip of tongue to soft palate)
Voiceless (no vocal chord vibration)	/p/	/t/	/k/
Voiced (vocal chord vibration)	/b/	/d/	/g/

These six phonemes are called "stop consonants" because they stop the flow of air producing the sounds. Three of the stops: /p/, /t/ and /k/, are usually voiceless — the vocal chords are not vibrated as they are produced. But they differ from each other in how the air is stopped: /p/ by bringing the lips together, /t/ by touching the tongue to the upper gums, /k/ by touching the tongue farther back on the soft palate. The other three stop consonants pair with the first three according to where they are stopped, but they are all usually voiced — the chords vibrate. So we have three pairs of phonemes that are alike except for a single difference: voicing.

Don't worry about the technical terms, however. The point is that you can easily confirm these differences by saying those sounds yourself and noticing what your lips and tongue do. The sounds that come to your ears are just enough alike and just enough different for your brain to perceive them as different phonemes. You've been using these differences in speaking and listening all your life, although this may be the first time you've examined them scientifically. As you learned to speak, you learned which differences to pay attention to and which ones to ignore.

Each language differs from other languages in which features separate phonemes. For example:

➤ In Tagalog, a language of the Phillipines, /p/ and /b/ form a single phoneme, whether voiced or voiceless.

➤ In Hawaiian and other Polynesian languages, /t/, /k/, /d/ and /g/, all stopped by the tongue, are part of a single phoneme. For example, the Hawaiian word *kapu*, meaning "forbidden," is the same as the Tahitian word *tabu*, which we've borrowed into English. They would be perceived as the same by speakers of these Polynesian languages.

➤ In English we perceive /l/ and /r/ as separate phonemes. In Japanese, however, the differences between them aren't significant, so Japanese speakers learning English have trouble distinguishing between English words like *rate* and *late*.

➤ Spanish uses <r> and <rr> in spelling to represent different phonemes. But since English doesn't have the second phoneme, *pero* (but) and *perro* (dog) sound the same to English speakers trying to learn Spanish.

➤ In different English dialects, the /r/ phoneme appears and disappears in varied contexts. John Kennedy's *Cuba* had an /r/ at the end (*Cubar*), particularly before words starting with vowels. Franklin Roosevelt's *fear* was /r/-less (*feah*).

All this is to demonstrate that phonemes are *perceptual constructs*. I'll refer frequently in this book to the ability of the brain to make sense of ambiguity, and to assign sound and graphic patterns to perceptual categories.

The ability our brains have to perceive things as different (or similar) even when they are very similar (or different) also applies to written language. When we come to examine letters and spelling patterns we'll see that we can also treat identical characters as different, depending on the contexts we find them in, and different ones as if they were the same. Even significantly different features can be perceived by the brain as essentially interchangeable.

Phonics

And that brings us to phonics, which isn't correctly a term applied to oral language at all, and one meaningful only in discussing languages that are written alphabetically. It refers to the *set of complex relationships* between phonology (the sound system of an oral language) and orthography (the system of spellings and punctuation of written language). (It is also used in teaching instruction to mean teaching about those relationships as part of teaching children to read, but for now we'll set that usage aside.)

The phrase "sound-symbol relationship" sometimes used in the professional literature implies that letters are symbols but sounds aren't. Of course that's not true; sounds are symbols as well, and phonics is the relationship between the two symbol systems. Sounds and letters have no meaning. The brain assigns meaning to individual phonemes within patterns of phonemes, and to letters within patterns of letters. Making sense of language, whether written or oral, is the business of the brain.

Graphophonics

Graphophonics is a term that represents a particular *combination of cues that readers and writers use*: the sound system (phonology), the graphic system (orthography), and the system that relates these two (phonics). In my reading miscue research I found that information from all three of these systems is used in the reading process.

We usually think of consonants in English as fairly regularly represented in spelling. But /f/, for instance, is spelled in several ways in different contexts: <f> in *five, fox, after*; <ff> in *off, office, cuff*; <ph> in *phonics, elephant, Ralph, sphere*; <gh> in *enough, laugh, cough*. All this is part of the complex phonics of English — and I haven't even mentioned special cases like *calf*, or *often* and *soften*, or one of the most common <f> words in English, *of*, which doesn't have the /f/ phoneme at all, but /v/ (*cup of coffee*). *Life* and *knife* become *lives* and *knives* as plurals, the shift from <f> to <v> nothing more than an arbitrary decision to shift the spelling with the sound. To keep it all straight, readers and writers have to employ orthographic information (spelling patterns), phoneme information, and the system of relationships between them.

It's unfortunate that phonics and these other terms are so often confused, even in the professional writing. We frequently hear this statement: "English is not a phonetic language" — which literally means that it uses no sounds! And substituting "phonic" doesn't help. What people usually mean is that English phonics is not a simple letter-sound system.

It's true that English phonics is more complex than many other European languages, but *no language has a pure set of one-to-one correspondences*. Phonics doesn't work that way. And though complex, English phonics isn't random or capricious as it's sometimes represented. There are rules; the trouble is they aren't simple and they vary from one dialect of English to another.

Non-alphabetic writing systems

I also want to call into question the simplistic misconception that the development of writing systems began with the earliest pictographs and found its perfection in modern alphabetic writing, a system superior to all others and fully sufficient to serve the needs of modern societies. Although this book is about phonics, which I've described as relevant only when discussing alphabetic writing systems, I want to point out briefly that non-alphabetic writing systems continue to serve important purposes and functions even in the modern world.

Alphabetic writing did evolve from non-alphabetic, and in general it works well for its users. However, non-alphabetic systems are better suited for some specific purposes. Our notions of how written language represents meaning mustn't be restricted to alphabetic writing. It's also important to understand and respect how well literacy works for those millions in the modern world who continue to use non-alphabetic writing systems.

The truth is that many writing systems exist in the world and many more were used in the past that aren't used now. The earliest forms of writing were not alphabetic. Alphabetic writing is believed to have originated in the Middle East and split into two main strands, one developing into the Greek and Roman alphabets and from there to modern European orthographies, including the cyrillic used in Russia and other Slavic countries, and the other moving into Asia through India and down through Malaysia.

Many of the world's most profound thoughts, philosophies and religious belief systems have been written about in non-alphabetic writing. Chinese uses characters that represent ideas. Japanese uses Chinese characters for the same ideas but adds a second systems of characters that represent the syllables of oral Japanese. These two systems are often mixed in writing Japanese, with content words represented in ideographic characters and function words in syllabic. Korea's move from a predominant use of Chinese characters to a syllabic system is relatively recent. Modern Hebrew and Arabic use alphabets historically related to Greek and Roman orthographies, but while consonants are fully represented in these languages, vowels are used only minimally. Some argue that these alphabets are really syllabic, since each letter represents the consonant and following vowels.

All of these modern writing systems work well for the societies that use them. It's widely reported, for example, that most Japanese children are well on their way to literacy before they start school, and the same is true in Taiwan, Hong Kong, Korea, Singapore and other parts of Asia.

The Chinese have chosen not to adopt alphabetic writing because they recognize an advantage in the fact that all people literate in the Chinese system derive the same meaning from the characters regardless of the oral language differences from region to region. Since the Chinese revolution, in mainland China the characters have been simplified and writing has shifted from the vertical right-to-left pattern to a horizontal left-to-right one. But an earlier plan to shift to pin-yin, their adaptation of the Roman alphabet, has been set aside for now, except for some use in early instruction.

Even in a basically alphabetic system, non-alphabetic elements are essential for many important functions. Maps and charts graphically represent information in much more compact and functional ways than alphabetic language can, for instance.

Mathematical notation

Perhaps the most abstract and complex ideas our modern civilization has developed can't be represented alphabetically in any efficient way. I'm talking about math and science. For example:

Numerals:	$1\,2\,3\,4\,5\,6\,7\,8\,9\,0$
Process signs:	$= + - \text{x} \; {}^{*} \div / \pm \sqrt{} < > \leq \geq \approx {}^{2} \; (\,)$
Other Symbols:	$\alpha \; \beta \; \pi \; \Sigma \; \sigma \; \% \; {}^{\circ}$

Virtually the entire world has adopted the same system of mathematical notation, in which each character represents not a sound but an idea or a mathematical concept. Remember when your teacher taught you that what we often call "numbers" are actually "numerals"? Numbers are the mathematical concepts or ideas that numerals represent. Numerals have names in each language, which we can spell alphabetically. But 1 stands for the same thing whether we call it *one, uno, un, een, einz,* or anything else. We call these common numerals Arabic, since they were discovered in India and brought back by Arab traders, first to the Moslem world and then to Europe.

When zero was invented some time later, we could combine the mathematical writing system with a base 10 (or other) number system and manipulate numbers by manipulating the numerals. We can also manipulate concepts by manipulating the graphic representation, because how the characters are arranged relates to their meaning (1 is one, but 11 is eleven). By using process signs we can write mathematical sentences (1 + 1 = 2) and create mathematical equations ($A = \pi r^2$) that compactly represent many complex relationships, functions and operations — and that are equally understandable to people all over the world who are literate in this non-alphabetic system.

In some cultures, Hebrew for instance, letters of the alphabet first doubled as numerals, the value of each being their place in the alphabetic order, but today those cultures use the same numerals and mathematical notions as the rest of the world. So you can haggle over the price of a purchase no matter where you go!

Science uses the same kind of ideographic notation system to represent complex formulas and operations, and manipulates concepts in the same way through graphic representation. Like math, science notation uses Roman and Greek letters to represent ideas or concepts, not sounds.

Computers, largely using base 8, greatly extend our capacity to do complex calculations and manipulations. Computer discs can even store music, videos and sensory data in the form of numerical codes to be translated back into sound, light and translated data. The keyboard I'm typing this on sends numerical codes to my computer to be stored and translated back into alphabetic writing on my screen, or to be sent to my printer which turns the numerical codes to alphabetic writing on paper.

Icons and logos

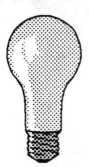

Icons and logos were once considered primitive forms of written language, but they've become very important in modern industrial society. By itself the light bulb icon here may not seem to mean much, but on a computer screen or above a character's head in a cartoon it speaks volumes.

The figure of a boy and bat will mean one thing as you pass a park and another as you walk through it.

THE UNIVERSITY OF

ARIZONA

TUCSON ARIZONA

The new University of Arizona logo caused a furor when it was released, partly because it cost some $30,000 to develop, and partly because students and alumni argued about how well it represented the University. Corporations often pay much more than my university did for a distinctive, eye-catching logo that will provide instant recognition and signify everything the corporation wants to represent to the viewers.

On computers, icons identify functions or processes that can be activated by means of a computer mouse. Icons prominently placed on packages give international freight handlers information they need for proper handling. A cracked glass says: "This is fragile." An arrow says: "This side up."

This strip of icons works well at the exit of a limited-access highway for motorists who need information readable at highway speeds: "At this exit you can find gas, parking, beverages and restaurants."

This icon is easy to read in context. When it's placed within a red triangle at the side of a highway passing through a wooded area, it tells drivers to watch for moose who may be crossing the road. I've seen similar signs for deer, cattle, kangaroos, koalas and even frogs. Other highway icons warn of railroads, curves, etc. On the road itself, lines tell us whether and where we can safely pass.

I saw this final icon first on the cover of a book, but I didn't get its meaning until I actually encountered it in its original Danish setting. At the end of the pier where a car-ferry docks it says very clearly: "Stop here or you and your car will fall in the sea." Danish print wouldn't have told me that!

Of course alphabetic writing is very important and very useful. But it's not the only or even necessarily the best system. It's one among many. It suits its users very well for some purposes, but not for all.

Alphabetically written language

In alphabetic languages, *patterns of letters* are used to represent *patterns of sounds*. That statement isn't just a complex way of saying that each sound is represented by a letter — that's not true, as I showed earlier. But there's a more fundamental reason why we must talk about patterns representing patterns: *oral language and written language work in quite different ways*.

Oral language is a stream of sound in *time*. When we speak, the particular order of sounds that we produce, in sequence, creates patterns of words and word parts, which are part of sentences, which are part of dialogues in a particular language in particular socio-cultural contexts. By making certain sounds follow others, we create grammatical patterns and assign meaning to oral language.

Surprisingly, the syntax (system of sentence patterns) of oral language is more complex than the syntax of written language. When we speak, we can vary stress, speed, loudness, pauses for breathing, and tones, as well as speech sounds. Each oral utterance has a complex contour. Questions have a different "tune" than statements. When we use complicated clause patterns, our intonation helps the listener untangle the grammatical dependencies. Our emotions are reflected in changes in pitch, in stress and in loudness. "Get out of here!" is a threat with one intonation and a friendly comment ("Stop teasing me!") with another.

Writing is different. The physical appearance of our words doesn't show our emotions. Intonation belongs to a whole sentence. Punctuation is marked only at specific points in the written text — and the puny exclamation point is no match for the force a speaker can give a statement! Writing is making marks on a flat, two-dimensional space. We produce written symbols or characters in some linear order to create a sequence that represents the grammatical patterns and meaning. But we can't represent as much in writing as in speech. Our punctuation can help readers organize the syntax and meaning of what they are reading, but we have to keep the structure simpler than what we use in speaking or our writing becomes incomprehensible.

To understand phonics scientifically we need to understand how the system of speech (phonology) works and how the system of writing (orthography) works, and then examine how the set of relationships between the two systems works (phonics). I'll examine the three systems in detail in the next chapters.

3

*Our
ability to
invent and use
language for social
purposes vitrually
defines our
humanity.*

Phonology: the sound system

All human societies possess language — our ability to invent and use language virtually defines our humanity. Two aspects of our nature make language both possible and necessary:

➤ We are a social species, dependent for our survival and well-being on our ability to form societies. The more complex societies become, the more interdependent individuals become.

➤ We are able to think symbolically. That is, we let *things* represent things and relationships between things.

We even let *relationships* represent relationships, *ideas* represent ideas, and *symbols* represent all of these, as well as other symbols. Our minds transfer relationships from one experience to another: analogy and metaphor extend meaning, thinking and language. And we create complex semiotic (sign) systems that enable us to express our thoughts about our experiences both to ourselves in reflective thinking and to each other in communication. Sometimes we use nonsense (meaningless symbols) to express sense. The only meaning symbols have is the meaning we give them.

Language: what a magnificent tool we humans have created by combining our social needs with our symbolic ability! And the language we've invented isn't simply a set of symbols, each with a separate meaning. It's a complete *system*, flexible and elastic enough to express any meanings we may need to, including some we haven't even thought of yet, meanings not only of things, but also of the relationships and interconnections that exist in our world. And though our language is complete, it's never finished. We've even invented conventions for how we might continue to invent language!

Creating language

When we were young, both as individuals and as societies, all we needed was oral language — except, of course, for those who couldn't hear and so had to invent a language they could produce with their hands and perceive with their eyes. In fact we all rely on our eyes as well as our ears for language. Both *visual signs*, made with body parts (notably hands and face), and *aural signs*, made by varying sound patterns, are used in all cultures.

As babies begin to produce speech sounds, they also produce hand and body signs (waving bye-bye, pointing, raising hands to be picked up, etc.), and most adults accompany their speech with hand motions and facial expressions. For the purpose of immediate social interaction, a combination of speech and body language is still easy, convenient, effective and usually sufficient. It was only as we matured and our needs became more complex that we began to need written language as well, so our thoughts and communications could be preserved over time and sent over distances.

Some people believe that the earliest oral words were onomatopoeic: the sounds things made became words for them, like babies calling trains "choo-choos" and dogs "bow-wows." All languages still have such words, like the English *whistle, tinkle, honk, toot, whip-poor-will*. But these words are just one example of our use of metaphor. We let characteristics of things represent them, and we borrow meanings of words from one set of relationships to another. We use flower names for women: Rose, Violet, Daisy. Nicknames like Slim, Shorty and Red describe a personal characteristic. And we shift meanings of words by analogy: a knife is sharp but so is a mind, a musical tone, or the taste of cheese; the weather is hot, but so is a form of jazz, a new product, a controversial issue, or a shade of pink. The contrast to hot jazz becomes cool jazz. Sharp minds contrast with dull ones. And so we continue to create new language by metaphor and analogy.

Oral language uses sounds as its symbol system. A single sound can represent a meaning, but it rarely does; usually we need sequences of sounds. A language must therefore have a grammar, a *system of sound sequences* complex enough to express all the complex meanings we need to deal with. Words and phrases must be created to bring the sounds together, so that entities and relationships of the real world can be represented.

Societies invent languages in much the same way individual children do. A one-year-old begins to say "ow-ow" whenever she sees a dog. For a time, all four-legged animals are "ow-ows," but eventually she moves toward the conventional category and only dogs are dogs. Consider what an achievement that is! The "simple" ability to see all dogs as dogs — small or large, shaggy or smooth, noisy or sleeping, etc. — shows the remarkably complex ability human beings have to use significant features for the creation of abstract categories.

We do also teach the concept of dog to our children, but we do it primarily by talking about the real dogs they meet until they form a category that matches our own. At the same time, the baby's "ow-ow" gives way to the conventional "dog" and her language becomes ever more and more complex and conventional as she thinks in more complex ways and communicates more and more successfully with those around her. Speaking and listening, reading and writing all employ the same human ability to form semantic and conceptual categories.

Language operates on several levels

Consider this short conversation:

Child: Mom, can I go out and play?
Mother: Yes dear, but don't cross the street.

A young preschool child wants to play outdoors. She knows she should ask permission and not just go out. She produces a stream of sound, but not just any sounds. She starts with her meaning: she has a request to make. She forms a question using the grammar and words her mother will understand. She chooses the sounds and appropriate intonation after she's decided on the grammar and wording.

But the child's focus is on her purpose and she's hardly aware of the process she goes through to ask her question. The mother hears the modulated sound stream and moves through the grammar and wording to get the meaning, all so easily that she has a sense of hearing the meaning. She understands the request and frames her cautionary answer, in turn going in rapid sequence from meaning to grammar and wording to sound stream.

We might think of language as a three-layered ball.

➤ The outer, most visible layer is the *symbolic* one; in oral language that's the phonemic system.

➤ Inside is the *lexico-grammatical* layer. The sounds of language are what reach our ears and they are the only part we can experience directly. The mother hears the patterns of sounds her daughter is producing, but she perceives them as patterns of phonemes organized according to the wording and grammatical patterns of the language.

➤ At the core is the meaning layer.

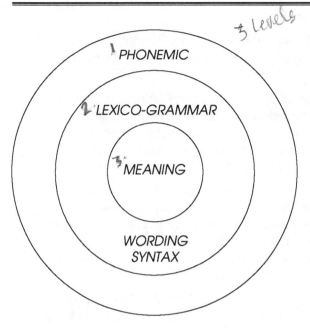

3 levels

PHONEMIC

LEXICO-GRAMMAR

MEANING

WORDING
SYNTAX

We must use the outer layers to comprehend or express meaning, but when the language is working well we feel as if we are seeing through the outer layers right to the meaning. We make speech noise to represent our meanings and we percieve that noise as language. Both mother and child feel as if they are directly exchanging meaning.

If the going gets tough, if we're having trouble making sense of what we're hearing, then the outer layers become opaque: we're aware of the details but not what lies beneath. If we can't understand language it's just noise. However, because we know the speaker is trying to be meaningful, we are likely to say, "I don't understand what you mean."

The smallest perceptual units in oral language are the *phonemes*. The little girl's sounds are determined by her meaning, her grammar and her wording. She says /kᵻn/ because *can* is an unstressed function word in her question. *Out and play* sounds like "outn play" because *and* is also unstressed. Her mother understands what she's saying because that's what she expects to hear. Both use their knowledge of the phonemes and intonation of English as they speak and listen.

Linguist Michael Halliday (1975) coined the term *lexico-grammar* for the second level of language, and he includes in this intermediate level the grammar of the language, its structure or system, and its vocabulary. The little girl's sentence has a common structure for questions in English. She begins with a verb marker, *can*, putting it in front of the subject of the sentence, *I*. (The statement form is: *I can go out and play*.) But her question also has rising pitch at the end. This intonation marks a lot of English questions.

Words, as combinations of morphemes, are the units of language that carry meaning, but only in grammatical, coherent text. Linguists use the term *morpheme* for minimal units of lanuage that can carry part of the grammatical or semantic information of the text — if phonemes are the atoms of language, morphemes are the molecules. The child's sentence happens to be composed of single-morpheme words. So is the mother's, except for *don't* which has two morphemes: *do* and *n't*.

Notice that the sound of the vowel in *do* changes in *don't*. The little girl already knows about that change — otherwise she couldn't understand her mother's caution.

Meaning, the third language level, like all aspects of language, is both personal and social. Each individual comes to assign meaning to the world in much the way that the surrounding culture does. Within the context of this conversation, "go out and play" has a social meaning shared by mother and child. Both have a sense of what kinds of activities will be included within "play."

Productive language always starts with meaning. Then the wording and grammar are assigned, and then the speaker produces a stream of sound with appropriate intonation. Listeners start with a sound stream, assign the wording and grammar, and then are able to make sense of the language. We may think we hear all the sounds as listeners, but that will be hard or easy depending on whether we have a sense of the meaning and grammar.

A good example is the telephone. Most messages we get easily. If we can't make out a name, however, we say, "Please spell it." But was that an /f/ or an /s/? "F, as in Frank," says the caller. In the military they developed words (able, baker, charlie, etc.) to make clear individual letters or radio signals. What these examples show is that our ability to perceive sounds is supported by our ability to make sense of what we hear. It's easy to repeat what we think we hear in a familiar language, but if the language is foreign to us we often can't even pick up the sounds we hear.

Languages don't need a large number of distinctly different symbols, just enough to create a sufficient number of different patterns to express all the different meanings we might want to express. Studies of the world's oral languages show that for a language to be effective it doesn't need to use a particular number of phonemes or all of the possible sound features. But the differences between the phonemes have to be perceivable.

What makes oral language possible, however, is that it doesn't have to be exact. A phoneme is not one sound but a whole range of sounds; no sound ever really exists by itself, but always in a sequence. To comprehend speech we don't require exact, precise speech. In fact, we can tolerate a great deal of ambiguity, even error. We are able to hear ranges of sounds produced by very different voices and yet perceive what is significant as the same, while ignoring the differences. We can even give the same sound or sound sequence different value or meaning in different contexts, as in these examples, where /ber/ is perceived as two different words: "The cave was bare; there was no bear in it" and "The bear couldn't bear the bee stings."

Perceiving language

The human brain is able to do remarkable things with bits of information the senses supply.

Seeing and hearing are strictly sensory. Sound and light have physical properties that affect sensors in our ears or eyes, which then send nerve messages to our brain. *The brain is the center of human perception.* It might sound silly to state such an obvious truth, but the fact is that we sometimes seem to consider the sensory organs as intelligent in themselves. Our eyes, ears, nose, tongue and skin are very important, of course. They provide our brains with sensory input. But they can't think. It's the brain that assigns significance, value and meaning to visual and aural information. What we see or hear is less important than what we *think* we see or hear. Perception is what the brain does with sensory input.

Piaget (1971) adds another insight: we see what we know. That is, we develop ways of organizing sensory information to get sense from it. If the eye seems to know where to look, if the ear seems to know what to listen for, it's because the brain has directed each to look or listen. Perception is always interpretive. It's surprising how little sensory information we actually need to perceive if we bring lots of other information to the task, and how much we need if we bring little. For example, even if I'm driving on a dark road late at night, I know when I'm approaching an intersection. How do I know? I see a dim stationary light that's gradually getting brighter, and that's all the sensory input I need. We often don't even know what small cues lead us to our conclusions. The human brain is able to do remarkable things with bits of information the senses provide.

That ability of the brain to make rich use of a little bit of sensory information is what makes language possible and enables it to work the way it does. The reason I call reading and writing processes *psycholinguistic* is that both *require thought as well as language.* If oral language required exact sound production and perception rather than some judgment by the brain, it would work far less effectively and far less efficiently.

Ambiguity is the key

Our language systems work as well as they do because the brain thrives on ambiguity and allows us to treat different sounds as the same and the same sounds, in different contexts, as different. In a well known experiment at Haskins Laboratory, people heard the same sound patterns as *gray ship, gray chip* and *great ship* as the researchers lengthened the sounds and the pauses between them (Cummings, 1988). But had the experimenters provided a fuller context with appropriate intonation, expectations would have led to more agreement by the listeners about what they heard. When a toothpaste commercial a few years ago claimed the product was "proved effective," some people heard "proved defective," perhaps based on their experience with that product!

Homophones are sets of words that sound the same but have different meanings. Our brain assigns the right meaning so easily in context that we're usually unaware that there were any other possibilities. And it rarely happens in actual discourse that two different meanings could fit the context.

Visual perception works much the same way, as we'll see in greater detail a bit later: different letter shapes can be perceived as the same and identical ones as different in different contexts. *Homographs* are look-alike words that have different meanings.

Sometimes the ordinary is so obvious we overlook it. If ambiguity truly complicated the process of making sense of language, we would, over time, eliminate it. But the ability of our brains to make the most of ambiguity is an intrinsic aspect of human language. Beginning with the early Greeks, scholars have argued about why language is so imperfect. The answer is obvious: language is a human invention that doesn't need to be perfect. Which means that we don't have to recognize every letter perfectly and match it accurately to a sound as we read. Our brains are too busy making sense of language to be bothered with that.

Perception is social, too

We develop language because we are social beings and language puts us in touch with others. The language we produce must therefore be comprehensible to others, and the language they produce must be comprehensible to us. As a result, we must agree on a broad range of common symbols and systems.

Language processes are *sociolinguistic* as well as psycholinguistic. Each social community has its own dialect, with sounds, words, idioms, even grammars that vary from those of other dialects. None of us simply speaks English. We have a home dialect, the form our family uses when we converse among ourselves, but we're also affected by the various communities we become part of. Every day TV brings into North American homes a number of regional and non-North American dialects. Even within one dialect people use several registers: one at home, another in school, another on the school playground, another in church, on the telephone, in public speaking, etc.

In the early 1960s our family moved to Detroit from Los Angeles, where my daughters went to Bagley Elementary School. Within a few months, their vowel in the <bag> syllable had shifted farther forward in the mouth and the word sounded almost like "Beygley" to me. I discovered that linguists had found this fronting, or migration forward, of vowel articulation in the mouth throughout a broad area of the Great Lakes region. It seemed most notable in the speech of girls and young women.

Language changes. My own view is that change comes about because each individual, as well as each generation, invents language all over again. While inventions always gravitate towards social conventions — they must for us to be understood by others — in the process, the conventions themselves are changed, sometimes a lot and quickly (as for slang) and sometimes in barely perceptible ways that slowly become evident over time.

In fact, every aspect of language changes over time. Think about the vocabulary used by the different generations in your own family. What do you call the machine you play musical recordings on: Victrola, gramophone, phonograph, record player, hi-fi, stereo, CD? Not only words but also idioms and metaphors fall in and out of style — the specific language of a 15-year-old movie will confirm that. The grammar and the sound systems of language also change over time. Language communities separated from each other will see their language grow apart. French in Canada is as different from Parisian French as American English is from the Queen's English.

Attention to features

Our ears sample from the stream of sound, always in context of trying to make sense of what we hear.

In theory a language should need only two symbols. Every natural language has more, of course, but at least two invented two-symbol languages have made significant contributions to human communication:

➤ *Morse code*, which became the basis of telegraphic and early radio communication, uses dots and dashes, short and long bursts of sound patterned by means of short and long pauses.

➤ *Binary computers* use open and closed switches, represented by just two numerals which, in varying patterns, can represent all possible numbers which, in turn, can represent the letters and special characters of written language systems.

Oral languages vary in the number of phonemes they use. Indo-European languages use around 40. The Polynesian languages of Hawaii, Tahiti, Samoa, etc. use only about 15. What limits the number of phonemes used is the number of ways the people of that culture produce and perceive sound differences. Any way that sounds can differ can be used to differentiate not only pairs of phonemes, but also sets of phonemes. In addition to the English /n/

sound, Spanish has its /ñ/, for example. Russian has two complete sets of consonants, hard ones like the /n/ and soft ones like the /ñ/. A soft sign is used to mark soft consonants in Russian spelling. When I studied Russian, my consonants tended toward the hard ones, which are more like English consonants.

Most languages differentiate some phonemes that other languages don't use at all. Some Africans use clicks made with the tongue as part of their language; Europeans may use the same clicks, but only for communicating with horses. Cantonese uses tone difference to produce phonemic differences. In English we use tone to create intonational patterns and grammar.

Linguists say that the number of phonemes a language uses and the phonetic features it does or doesn't use to produce the phonemes are arbitrary. It's as if each society had set out to invent its own language, arbitrarily deciding which of the endless number of available phonemes would be used. In a way that is what happened: the early users of each language created it over long periods of time. And those of us who use the language now keep inventing, reinventing and reshaping it.

When we learn our first language, we learn two important things: what to pay attention to and what not to pay attention to. We learn to pay attention to the distinctive features of speech sounds (the phonology) our own language uses while ignoring the features it doesn't use. What makes learning a second language difficult is that we have to learn to pay attention to phoneme features we earlier learned to ignore. English speakers hear the difference between the Spanish /r/ and /rr/, but perceive them as the same. Spanish speakers hear the difference between the English /d/ and /th/, but treat them as one phoneme because the Spanish /d/ sits in between the two English phonemes.

Allophones

Phonemes in a given language usually have several variant forms, used in different places and in specific sequences of sounds. Those variant forms are called *allophones*.

In English, for example, the /p/ in *spin* and the /p/ in *pin* are different. If you put your hand in front of your mouth and say those two words, you'll feel a burst of air from the one but not from the other. You'll feel the same difference in *kin* and *skin*. The phonemes with the burst of air are *aspirated*, the others *unaspirated*. We never use the aspirated form of a phoneme after /s/.

On the other hand, we never use the unaspirated form at the beginning of a word, although the French do. We say *Paris* with an aspirated /p/, while the French /p/ is closer to our unaspirated form. Linguists say that the allophones of a phoneme are in "complementary distribution" — that is, each variant form has its own place and never occurs in the places of the other forms. We learn which one to use quite naturally, but we treat them perceptually as the same. Young children learning to talk will produce the right allophone of /p/ in *spin* even when they can't yet produce the /s/ that comes before it!

The features we use to perceive the distinct phonemes of oral language are very important — linguists call them "distinctive" features because we use them to tell one phoneme from another. And here is the puzzler that shows how truly efficient human perception is: listeners must ignore the differences between allophones of a particular phoneme, /p/ for example, and at the same time notice the features those allophones share. We must perceive the two forms of /p/ in *pin* and *spin* as the same, though they are not.

The problem is, if we had to identify each successive phoneme we hear and attend to every feature of every sound, we would never comprehend speech. Fortunately, our brain takes charge as we listen. Guided by what our brain knows about the phonological system, our ears sample from the stream of sound, always in the context of trying to make sense of what we're hearing. While we are preoccupied with meaning, our brain searches for the most useful aural cues, predicting what we will hear as it is making sense of the language.

Only when meaning is lost do we ask ourselves: "What was that I heard?" Or we say: "Sorry, I didn't catch what you were saying." Our clever brain uses only enough information to make sense. It detects the tiniest of differences and ignore the grossest, whatever it takes in a particular context.

Why am telling you all this, more than you may really care to know about the sounds of language? I have two major reasons:

➤ We need to appreciate what kids demonstrate to us they know when they use language. Everyone, child or adult, who can produce comprehensible speech and understand the speech of others is showing control over the sound system of the language. *There is no need to teach children "their sounds"; they learned them as they learned to talk.*

➤ We need to understand the workings of phonology as a basis for recognizing how this complex oral language system is related to the complex orthography of the written language through a complex phonics.

To be honest, I have a third reason as well:

➤ I hope that all this scientific information may help to demystify phonics and dispel the myths that surround the teaching and learning of it.

I'll talk in detail later about how letter patterns relate to sound patterns. Just for now, this one point illustrates the complexity: as sounds have allophones, so letters have variant forms we can call *allographs* — upper and lower case forms, for instance. So when we talk about phonics as letter-sound correspondences, we're really talking about relating abstract symbols from two systems, symbols which have many alternate actual forms and which are distributed quite differently in each system.

Sounds in context

Speech sounds never occur by themselves, but always in a stream of sound. The previous example of /p/ in *pin* and *spin* drew attention to the role the mouth plays in producing adjacent sounds. To create particular sounds, the lips are relaxed or tensed, the tongue is lifted, pulled back, or touched to the teeth, and the shape of the oral cavity is changed. But getting the tongue into the new position required for changing from one sound to another requires travel, so that any sound may be altered depending on what phoneme precedes or follows it. (Letters vary in cursive writing for the same reasons.)

Here are some examples:

➤ Vowel sounds are changed by the consonants that precede and follow them. This is particularly true with /r/ and /l/.

➤ Vowels also change when they are unstressed. We often use this stress contrast in English to differentiate related verbs and nouns: *recess/recess, process/procession, contest/contest, abstract/abstract, intern/intern*.

➤ Some sounds almost disappear in certain sequences, like the /t/ in *wanted* or *counted*. In most North American dialects this /t/ is nasalized and virtually disappears. We say *west* with a /t/, but lose that sound in *westside*. Sometimes the differences between distinct sounds disappear in specific contexts: listen to *ladder* and *latter*, which sound the same in most North American dialects of English. Notice that the /t/ in *later* also usually moves to a /d/.

➤ Speech sounds vary in how long we take to produce them. The /t/ in *stick* is so short that we can't separate it from the sounds before and after.

Phonemes are mental abstractions to which we assign sensory input; they are schemas our brains can use to turn the sounds we hear into the symbol system of oral language. We "hear" what we expect to hear and assign phonemic values on the basis of what we've learned about the phonemes of the language. We believe we hear a /t/ in *wanted, latter* and *stick* because we "know" it's there.

Morphophonemics

Linguists use the term *morpheme* for the smallest unit of the oral language that can carry meaning and/or grammatical information. A morpheme is composed of one or more phonemes. In English there are very few morphemes with less than two phonemes.

"Free morphemes" can stand by themselves, while "bound morphemes" must always be associated with other morphemes. *A, the, train, forest, carnival* and *salamander* are words composed of single morphemes even though they vary in number of syllables. Words may also be composed of a combination of free and bound morphemes.

House is a single morpheme. We can compound it to make words containing two single morphemes: *doghouse, greenhouse, lighthouse, outhouse, boathouse, houseman, houseboat*. We can form its plural by adding a bound morpheme, /+z/, to make *houses*. In my American dialect, that changes the /s/ in *house* to /z/, however, and the same change occurs when I use *house* as a verb. *Housing, houses, housed* require bound morphemes to be added to the base, in each case changing the /s/ to /z/. But note that we retain the <s> in all the spellings.

Another pair of words where the consonant changes between noun and verb is *bath* and *bathe*. The <e> is added to mark the vowel change. But in the plural of the noun the consonant sound also changes in some dialects, certainly for me: *They take baths*. This example also demonstrates how speech sounds change in the context of different sound sequences. Linguists call this *morphophonemics*: changes in phonemes as morphemes come together.

English vowels shift to schwa (/ə/) when the word or syllable they are in is unstressed. The /o/ in the noun *compress* becomes a schwa when the accent shifts in the verb. In changing from *confide* to *confidence*, both vowels shift as the accent shifts, the first from the schwa and the second to the schwa.

Here are some examples of consonant phonemes changing as morphemes come together: *please* → *pleasure, press* → *pressure, rite* → *ritual, race* → *racial, rate* → *ratio, fact* → *faction* → *factual, grade* → *gradual, revise* → *revision, louse* → *lousy*. Notice also the vowel changes in some of these words. You can discover similar changes in *educate, tissue, treasure, leisure, nation, azure* and *fissure*, for instance. And because speech is a stream of sound, the same kind of changes can take place across word boundaries as well: *would you* becomes *woujya; can't you* becomes *canchya*.

These examples can't be dismissed as a small number of phonemic "irregularities." Such morphophonemic shifts are necessary in all oral languages, but since we learn them without thought when we learn to talk, they seem so natural that most of us are unaware of how common they are. They are all rule-governed, however, and don't represent lazy or careless speech. Saying *canchya* represents an appropriate application of specific morphophonemic rules. (Feel free to use this last sentence on the next person who criticizes your "sloppy speech." Then top it off with a "Gotcha!")

Dialect differences

If each letter represented a sound, then the spelling of each dialect group would have to be unique.

Each dialect sounds different from every other dialect of the same language, and all languages are really families of dialects. Replicating a study I did of reading miscues of American children speaking different dialects of English, Osuna (1990) did a study of children speaking five of the dialects of Spanish spoken in Venezuela.

She found the children's Spanish dialects represented in their oral reading just as I had found the dialects of the English-speaking children in my study influencing their reading. In neither case was that a problem. The readers could make sense of the written language even when it didn't match their dialect. And spelling, as we'll discuss later, was shown to be constant across dialects in both English and Spanish.

I pronounce *marry, merry* and *Mary* the same way. How about you? I also pronounce both *witch* and *which* with no /h/ before the /w/. My *fear* has a distinct /r/, unlike Roosevelt's *feah*. My *Cuba* has no /r/, unlike Kennedy's. I've heard *almond* pronounced at least four different ways. My *al* has the vowel sound found in *hot* and a distinct /l/. Other people use the vowel sound in *pal*, with an /l/. Still others use either vowel sound with no /l/. Almond growers in Northern California relish the local joke that when the nuts fall from the tree they get the /l/ knocked out of them!

A third-grade boy in southern Indiana asked his teacher (she heard), "How do you spell rat?" "R-a-t," she said. "No ma'am", he responded, "I don't mean *rat* mouse. I mean *right* now." My *light, might, right, sight, tight* and *night* all rhyme with *bite*. Appalachian kids in a research study I did rhymed them with *hot*. When they read the phrase *light bulb* in a story, it sounded to me like *lot bu'b*. In some Scottish dialects of English, the same words evoke a throaty consonant before the final /t/ similar to the Spanish phoneme in *Xavier* and *Mexico*. In Australia, on the other hand, *might* is a homophone for *mate*.

The most common Canadian dialect of English is very similar to my Midwestern US dialect. One exception is the vowel in words like *out* and *house* which seem to me to have the vowel of my *boot* rather than my *bout*.

For those of you who have found your way of saying certain words put down by others, here's a vignette, told to my wife Yetta by a principal when she was discussing a student teacher with him:

"Mary Beth is doing very well, but I wish you'd help me figure out how to help her with her speech problems. For instance, she says 'pitcher' when she means 'picture.' I tried to show her. I said, 'See, this is a pitcher and that on the wall is a picture.' And she said, 'No, sir, those are homophonous in my dialect.' I couldn't go any farther. I don't even know what homophonous means."

Yetta explained that her students took linguistics courses and that Mary Beth, from rural Michigan, had recently learned to attend to and appreciate her own dialect.

If it were possible for each letter in written English to consistently represent a single phoneme, then logically the spellings of each dialect group would look as unique as their speech sounds. But most languages have opted to standardize spellings across dialects. *Almond* is the standard spelling regardless of the varied ways different dialect communities say it.

I'll deal later with the impact standardized spellings across dialects has on phonics and using phonics in teaching reading. It's sufficient here to point out that phonics, the relationships between the sound system of oral language and the orthography of written language, must vary from dialect to dialect if spelling is to be standardized. And that means there can be no standard phonics across all dialects. If, as the song says, "I say 'tomayto' and you say 'tomahto,'" then our phonic values are different. If bin and been sound the same to me, bin and Ben to someone else, bean and been to a third person, and bean and being to a fourth, then phonics must vary from dialect to dialect.

Of course, we could pretend that dialect differences don't exist, or that everybody else is wrong and must learn to speak the way I do. Some people advocate just that. I won't. And even if I did, it wouldn't make the differences go away! Although some people believe that mass communication (TV, radio, and movies) will serve to eliminate dialect differences, studies like those by William Labov (1972) don't support that assumption. In fact, they seem to show that differences continue to develop.

Intonation

Knowing what to do as you use language is very different from knowing about language.

Oral languages have what amounts to a rhythm, a beat or a tune. We create intonation contours for the language using variations in pitch, in stress and in pause patterns.

Listen to the difference between the statement "That boy is John" and the question "That boy is John?" I can give the question a different meaning by stressing the first word: "*That* boy is John?" (not the other one?), and a different one still if I stress the second word: "That *boy* is John?" (I thought he was a man).

By using subtle voice variations, I can make complex sentences that have several clauses easy for my listeners to follow because my intonation makes clear the various dependencies and references of the sentence parts. Writing uses punctuation to do some of the things that intonation does in oral language. However, written language has to be less complex in its clause structure, because punctuation is less flexible than intonation.

Some years ago I thought I had invented an easy way to write an article. I would write an outline, then talk the body into a tape recorder and ask a secretary to type the finished work. Alas, my sentences were so complex and my clauses so intertwined that I had to spend a lot of time reworking the typed material to make it comprehensible. Sometimes I had to go back to the tape myself to figure out what I'd said! It took me much longer to edit than it would have to write the article directly. Intonation makes it possible to use much more complex constructions in oral language than in written.

Stress

We know that vowels in unstressed syllables change their sounds to schwa. And we know that word stress can be used in English to differentiate noun and verb forms of the same word: *contest/contest,* for example. Function words like *the, is, some, was, to* are also usually unstressed. Nothing in English spelling represents these changes, however; we don't mark stress on vowels as the Spanish and French do. Sometimes we do use an apostrophe to mark where the vowel disappears altogether in unstressed contexts, as when /not/ becomes /nt/ in words like *don't* and *isn't.*

Stress also helps listeners to assign a syntactic pattern to what they hear. There are several levels of stress in English, with complex rules for how we assign levels as we speak. Each sentence has one or more major stresses, for example. In writing, we use such devices as <u>underlining</u>, **boldface** or *italics* to indicate unusual stress, but we have no system in our writing that corresponds to the normal sentence stress patterns of oral English. Readers infer and assign a stress pattern as they read orally.

Pitch

Some languages, such as Cantonese, use pitch differences phonemically: sounds at different pitch levels may be different phonemes. Words that otherwise sound alike are differentiated by Chinese listeners by their pitch patterns — one reason, perhaps, why Europeans think they hear a "sing-song" pattern when they hear Chinese dialects spoken.

In English we use pitch also to indicate the syntactic structure. In most English dialects, the most common sentence pattern ends with a falling pitch, while questions usually end with a rising pitch. In fact, virtually any English statement can be changed to a question by changing the pitch pattern. In dialogue a speaker may question the truth of a statement by repeating it with a changed pitch: "Mary ate the whole thing." . . . "Mary ate the whole thing?"

You could easily have repeated that sentence as a question, using a different pitch, even if you'd never once thought about how pitch differs. There's a big difference between knowing what to do as you use language and knowing *about* language. Halliday (1975) found that his infant son Nigel was using intonation to represent function as he was learning to talk. His "Daddy shoes" was sometimes a comment — "Those are Daddy's shoes." — and sometimes a question or request — "Are those Daddy's shoes?" or "Give me Daddy's shoes." That's a perfect illustration of the way all aspects of language are learned. We learn to control the features and rules of language as we attempt to use language, and we don't need to learn *about* language to use it.

Juncture or pause

The third aspect of intonation we use in oral language is juncture or pause. We have a sense that we pause between sentences. We also tend to think that we pause at points within sentences, though for relatively shorter times. Actually we use a whole contour of stress, pitch and pause at sentence ends; the pauses themselves may be very short or even non-existant.

People often equate the intonation contours between sentences with periods (or question marks and exclamation points), and commas with shorter, within-sentence pauses. But we have to breathe when we talk, and we can't always make our breathing coincide with pause patterns. Patterns of pitch, stress and pause are all relative. The pause at the end of a sentence may be longer than any within the sentence but shorter than the pauses at the end of other sentences. Similarly, the heavy stress in one sentence may not be as heavy as some secondary stresses in others. And most of this, children have learned how to do before they come to school.

Intonation contours

One reason each aspect of intonation is so variable is that pitch, stress and juncture work together, providing a continuous contour for each sentence and for whole dialogues. Intonation is called "super-segmental" by linguists because the intonation contour rides above the whole sequence and can't be directly related to the particular segments (phonemes) in any one-to-one way. In written language we put punctuation marks at specific points. Intonation and punctuation have similar purposes: to help listeners/readers assign syntactic patterns. But they don't really correspond in any useful way. Punctuation doesn't give the reader very much of the information that intonation provides the listener. We must infer much of that information during reading, and writers must be careful not to make the reader's job too hard.

Just to complicate this further, intonation also varies from dialect to dialect. In Black English and Hawaiian Pidgin, for example, you can replace stress by elongating the vowel in a word. "Goooood" is a lot better than "good." The use of contractions is also related to intonation, as the rhythm of a dialect may require the shortening of some syllables. I'm convinced that one thing that makes unfamiliar dialects of one's own language hard to understand is that the unfamiliar intonation contour makes it hard to predict and assign a syntactic pattern. Once we "tune in" to the new dialect it becomes easier to understand and the differences seem less extreme.

Summary

If we remember that phonic relationships in English are between patterns of sounds and patterns of spelling, then we can see that sound features, dialect differences and intonation have a major effect on phonic relationships in any given context. Vowels change, grammar is shifted, and the "sound" of the whole determines the grammar and meaning in ways that the orthographic system can't fully represent. By pulling language apart and teaching kids letter-sound or isolated-word phonics strategies, we distort all these complex relationships. That's another reason why phonics can be learned only in the context of using it in real language.

4

*It is our
human sense-
making ability that
shapes our use of the
visual and phonic
information we
receive.*

Orthography: the written symbol system

Now I want to explore how English orthography, the second prong of graphophonics, works. That term used to refer to "good spelling," and it was a school subject. (There's also a word that means "bad spelling": *cacography*. Since *cacophony* means "bad sounds," can you guess what *cac* means in Greek?) But when linguists and others, myself included, needed a term to describe *the whole of the system of written language,* including punctuation and special features like italics, underlining, boldface, capitalization, etc., the meaning of orthography was broadened. I use the term in its broad sense here, as a set of writing tools for making meaning.

Orthographic tools

Alphabets

Our 26-letter alphabet is a variation of the Roman one. Most modern Western European languages also use the Roman alphabet, with modifications to fit the particular sound patterns of the language. Spanish and French use accent marks over vowels, for example. Scandinavian languages add some vowel letters. English uses letter combinations like <th>, <sh>, <ch> and <ph> to represent single sounds.

We all use the Roman alphabet because of Rome's lengthy domination of Western Europe. For similar historical reasons, some European languages are written in more than one alphabet. A common Slavic language in Yugoslavia is written in Cyrillic by Orthodox Serbs and other Slavs, in the Roman alphabet by Catholic Croatians. When Europeans, notably the British, invaded India, they discovered many different alphabets in use by various ethnic groups. It's ironic that India, with a long history of alphabetic literacy that predates the coming of Europeans, now has a high level of illiteracy.

European Jews use the Hebrew alphabet to write Yiddish, a Germanic language they carried into Eastern Europe when they were driven out of the Rhine valley during the Crusades. North African and Middle Eastern Jews use Hebrew characters to write the Spanish-based Romance language Ladino, which they carried into North Africa and the Middle East when they were expelled from Spain in 1492. A dialect of French in Provence was also written with the Hebrew alphabet.

Missionaries have tended to use the alphabet of their religion's early language in creating writing systems for converted people, each alphabet modified as required. Some of the native languages of the far north in North America are written in Cyrillic because of early Russian Orthodox missionaries. The Mormons actually developed their own alphabet and used it for a while in their conversions of supposedly preliterate people. These days the Wycliff Bible translators are the world's most active group in developing orthographies for missionary use.

It's clear from all this that the choice of alphabets has been a matter of fairly arbitrary historical/cultural decision-making. In the case of orthographies, the choices reflect who had political power and/or cultural prestige at the time the decisions were made. Theoretically, any number of writing systems could be adapted to serve the purposes of any particular language.

Writing implements

Some characteristics of writing systems are determined by the nature of writing itself and of the materials it employs in any time and place. With few exceptions, we now use smooth flat surfaces to write on, and we mark with ink, chalk or other soft material such as charcoal, graphite, etc.

Throughout history, however, the forms writing has taken have been influenced by the media at hand. The Babylonians used wedge-shaped styluses to press their characters into soft clay, so cuneiform characters show wedge shapes. In the Middle Ages scribes used quills and ink on parchment or paper, producing letter forms that depended on the quill's ability to create lines thicker or thinner, in much the same way that Chinese calligraphers still do. Medieval manuscripts were "illuminated" by colorful, ornate pen and brush designs.

When printing presses began to be used, the need to cast type influenced the shapes of letters and other symbols, producing writing that looked very different from the cursive writing forms that had already developed in many writing systems. Modern computers now produce infinite variations in size, slant, height, thickness, darkness, or any other characteristic of print at the flick of a key or the touch of a mouse button. Computers even simulate handwriting, and allow us to produce non-alphabetic symbols — icons, logos and other graphics — even if we don't possess any artistic ability.

Over the centuries, forms of writing such as calligraphy, italics, fancy handwriting and elegant fonts were developed to convey beauty and subtle non-alphabetic meaning. We can make documents look official, spiritual, commercial, amorous, vulgar, informal, intimate, snobbish, rustic or uncouth simply by our choice of fonts and/or handwriting. Of course these outcomes reflect cultural perceptions as well.

Using the tools

How do alphabets and physical tools for producing writing shape the writing system in the hands of writers and readers? Simply speaking, orthographies must be producible by writers and perceivable by readers. The two don't always work well together. Cursive writing can be produced more easily and rapidly by writers than disjointed letter forms, but it's often less legible. Each of us develops a personal handwriting but our handwritings are not equally "reader friendly."

Writing from the point of view of the writer

Many cultures have employed *scribes*, a small but highly skilled group of people who have often enjoyed special religious status or political power. Among the Maoris, the men who carve the totems must spend many years learning the genealogy of their clans, because their works record that history. Among the Navajos, it's the medicine men who produce the intricate sand paintings that communicate with the powerful spirit world. The chief scribes in charge of the hieroglyphics on the tombs in ancient Egypt were important politically.

In each of these cases the complexity of the writing system is unimportant: since few people do the writing, few need to possess the skills and knowledge writing requires. But as a society needs more writers, writing has to become more manageable and easily learned.

As written language became more important, people looked for ways of producing multiple copies of books and documents without having scribes tediously duplicate them. So, first the Chinese and then the Europeans invented a printing press and movable type. People who say that Gutenberg's invention of the printing press made mass literacy possible have things backwards; it was society's need for more literate people and therefore more copies of books that required the invention of the printing press. As the need for more universal and faster writing developed, the typewriter was invented. Now computers, word processors and electronic printers have replaced much of the earlier technology.

Orthographies must have characteristics that enable individuals to master and use them quickly. The Chinese have developed thousands of characters, but a few hundred account for 99% of their writing. A relatively small number of strokes are combined in *radicals*, or root forms, which in turn combine to produce characters. Words with related meanings share common radicals. This orthography works well for Chinese writers.

Alphabetic writing systems also use a limited number of letters composed of a small set of repetitious strokes. One would think that as our writing systems changed over time, greater efficiencies would have evolved for writers. That's happened to some extent, but it's produced more rather than less ambiguity for readers.

Differences between letters have sometimes diminished to the point of disappearing. Are these characters the same or different: 1, I, l? On my computer keyboard the first is the numeral one, the others the capital of the ninth and the lower case of the twelfth letters of the alphabet, but on paper they look very much the same. There's no ambiguity in this sentence, however: "I'll see you at *101 Dalmatians* tonight, OK?" In context, we easily disambiguate any ambiguous graphemes. In fact, we likely aren't aware of the potential problem in deciding which letter/numeral is which.

In the 1930s some people became concerned that cursive writing was too difficult for beginning writers to learn. So a new initial manuscript orthography was developed, a "manuscript" form composed essentially of sticks and balls — a form that's still common in North America until second or third grade when the transition to cursive is made. Advocates believed that this orthography would also facilitate reading, since it looked more like print fonts. In fact, primers and preprimers began to be printed in a similar font. It was introduced without much research support, however, and there has been little research to support it's continued use.

On the other hand, most primary teachers are convinced that starting with manuscript makes learning to write easier, and there's no strong evidence that they are wrong. Substitute teachers in early grades are sometimes told by pupils, "We can read reading but we can't read writing yet." In any case, transition to cursive writing is not a prolonged or difficult process for most pupils. In fact, the more recent D'Nealian writing, a manuscript form with added extensions that make it look more like cursive, has become popular for easing that transition.

Other cultures have also introduced "learning" orthographies. Most Japanese children start school with only syllabic writing, adding characters derived from Chinese later. China has recently begun some use of pin-yin, an alphabetic writing, for beginners. And in the teaching of Hebrew and Arabic, vowel marks are often added to the regular characters for beginners. When you think about what beginners learn from print in their environment, however, it's apparent that these accomodations aren't really necessary.

Ironically, many adult writers (like me) have adopted manuscript writing in deference to family, friends and colleagues who have told us what they think of our cursive handwriting. In fact, my grades as an undergraduate improved when I began writing essay exams in manuscript. These days, of course, most people use typewriters or word processors to produce more acceptable, readable letters and papers.

Writing from the point of view of the reader

We have the remarkable ability to treat major differences in letters as irrelevant and minor ones as significant, while at the same time making sense of the print.

Orthography must be legible for readers to be able to make sense of it. Some features of writing systems, particularly alphabetic ones, clearly have readers in mind. Separating words by extra space is an obvious example. It should be noted, however, that for many centuries readers got along without that feature. Word space in writing with Roman characters is a relatively late invention; in earlier times, English used alternate letter forms at the ends of words. In Chinese and Japanese writing, the characters are equally spaced whether one or two or more together are needed to represent a word. Clearly, readers are capable of predicting and assigning their own word boundaries.

Print must also be large enough to be seen by the human eye. When contracts, warranties or product warnings use print so small that we literally can't read them, we suspect the writer's motive. And, of course, the older we get, the larger the print we seem to need. There must be enough contrast between the print and its background for features of letters to be distinguished. And it helps if print fonts are familiar and spellings close to conventional, or plausible inventions. More about that later.

While handwriting will be harder for most readers than print, the amount of difficulty we have will depend on our knowledge of the content and our familiarity with the writer — that is, any particular example of writing will be hard or easy to read depending on what the reader brings to the reading. We can get used to some otherwise illegible writing if it belongs to family or friends. I once had a colleague whose handwriting was so hard to read that even his secretary couldn't decipher it. I could often figure out passages for her, however, because he and I had co-authored a book and shared a lot of knowledge and schemas. I would use the surrounding text to predict and infer what he was probably saying, and then look for visual cues in the writing itself to confirm my inferences.

Americans often notice common characteristics of handwriting among the British, and an English colleague pointed out to me some common features of American handwriting. Cultural handwriting differences and similarities are akin to dialect differences in speech, although there may be school influences as well. My wife's handwriting is almost identical to her older sister's. Their immigrant mother, alarmed at immaturities in Yetta's developing handwriting, had her copy her sister's writing for a nickel a page!

Reader-writer tradeoffs

Obviously, tradeoffs will develop between a writer's orthography and a reader's orthography. Look-alike letters don't need to be eliminated because, in context, readers will know whether 1, I or l is intended. Handwriting can become uniquely stylized and still be readable, since readers have considerable tolerance for ambiguity.

Again modern technology gives us some interesting insights. The task of office scanners, for example, is not unlike the perceptual task required of human readers. We recently acquired a scanner ourselves. With the proper optical character recognition (OCR) software, it's supposed to be capable of turning any printed page into word processor input, even preserving the line and paragraph formatting. We wanted it particularly to scan some old articles so we could edit them for republishing, and I'm pleased to report that our first effort with it produced a roughly 98% accurate character recognition.

In the first articles we scanned, the computer sometimes misjudged 1 and l, but not 0 and O. (See, out of context you're not sure which is which either!) It made some mistakes human readers would be very unlikely to make: <d> changed to <cl>, for example, but only some of the time. It also sometimes mixed up <h> and <n>. Hyphens at the ends of lines were a problem, since they could be performing either of two functions: separating syllables of the same word or indicating compounds. The scanner solved the problem by putting a space in place of the hyphen, so what came before and after the hyphens became separate words. Fortunately, a spellcheck caught most of the non-words the scanner produced.

Here's an unedited passage exactly as it was scanned:

Traffic signs and commercial logos, the most functional and situationally embedded written language in the environment, are learned easily and early (Good man & Goodman, in press). Despite their differences and history of acquisition, oral- ancl written-language processes become parallel for those who become liter ate; language users can choose the process that better suits their purposes. Readers may go from print to meaning in a manner parallel to the way they go from speech to meaning.

Since the deep structure and rules for generating the surface structure are the same for both language mocles, people learning to read may draw on their con trol of the rules and syntax of oral language to facilitate developing proficiency in written language. This is not a matter of translating or recoding print to sound and then treating it as a listening task. Rather, it is a matter of readers using their knowledge of language ancl their conceptualizations to get meaning from print, to develop the saml)ling, predicting, confirming, and correcting strategies parallel to tl-ose they use in listening. Gibson and Levin (1975) seem to agree with us that recoding print to souncl is not necessary for adults, and Rader (1975) finds that it is not even necessary for chilclren.

Clearly the human programmers have built in algorithms for handling most of what readers must do. While the scanner doesn't have to make sense of the document, it does have to go beyond one-to-one character matching and make some use of context in choosing between alternatives. Notice that there were several <cl> for <d> misperceptions, but a lot of times <d> came through fine, many more times than they were misperceived — and notice there was no <d> for <cl>. There was a *l)* for <p> and a *l-* for <h>, but the only problem otherwise was end-of-line hyphens in the original setting. Although not in this sample, in the rest of the scanned text a few problems occurred with <n> as well.

Hurrah for the machine!

And double hurrah for human readers who not only demonstrate even better perception, but also make sense of print at the same time as they "scan" with their own "optics." (Very few readers would have trouble reading this scanner-produced material with all its errors. And incidentally, the scanner bombed totally on a script font.) In fact, it will be the core of my argument that it is *our sense-making ability as readers that makes possible our superior use of visual and phonic information.* We tolerate far more ambiguity than machines because we are constructing meaning at the same time.

Allographs

As *allophones* are alternate forms of phonemes, so *allographs* are alternate forms of graphemes: the individual perceptual units that writing produces. There is no one <h> that is *the* <h>; what there is, is a variety of allographs that readers must perceive as being the same although they're not.

The following examples show the four ways I normally write <h>, four because I use manuscript form as often as I use cursive.

$$\mathcal{H},\ \hbar,\ H,h$$

My computer printer can produce many more allographs of <h> — H h *H h* H h *H h* H h, for example — and I can read still more.

Everyone who reads can recognize scores of alternative forms of each letter. Variations may be large or small. In print they will depend on the font in use; in cursive writing, on what characters precede and follow. We treat all these allographs as the same letter, although we use different perceptual information to identify and produce them. Like allophones, allographs are also in complementary distribution — that is, capitals can occur only in locations where small letters are not permitted. And we would rarely mix fonts within a single word.

The scanner also has to cope with allographs, adjusting its algorithms to fit very different fonts. Some fonts are easier for a scanner to read than others, but the success rate in most cases is very high. In fact my OCR program is clever enough to select a more or less matching font from my laser printer driver as it deposits the transformed book or journal text into a WordPerfect file for me to edit.

Even so, human readers are better at dealing with differences than scanners are. They have the remarkable ability to treat major differences in letters as irrelevant and minor ones as significant, *while making sense of the print*. I've documented thousands of misperceptions in reading: readers thinking they saw one word or phrase when they actually saw another. But these misperceptions are very different from my scanner's miscues. They are constrained by the reader's search for meaning.

One reader made two miscues in this passage:

> *while   always*
> when I am away cutting wood.

Beyond the graphic similarity between the observed and expected responses, we note that all of the words make sense in the reader's construction of meaning.

English spelling

Consistent spellings help readers and writers hang onto the meaning patterns of related words.

How often have you heard it said in various ways: English spelling is extremely complex, even capricious? That belief has shaped these common-sense conclusions:

➤ Reading difficulty largely results from the complexity of English spelling.

➤ Reforming English spelling will make it more consistent and predictable.

➤ Reforming spelling will make phonics work better and eliminate reading difficulties.

I don't agree with those conclusions, and in this section I want to demonstrate why.

It seems natural to relate spelling patterns to sound patterns in alphabetically written languages. But I've shown that it's a gross oversimplification to say that letters represent sounds. Let's explore the reality of English in more detail.

In the word *man*, the letters do, in fact, seem each to represent a single sound. Each successive letter <m> <a> <n> can be related to a phoneme of the oral word /m//ae//n/. Furthermore, this spelling fits into a common spelling pattern that includes rhyming words like *pan, can, tan, fan* and *van*, as well as *map, mat* and *mad*, which vary in the final sound. So, there appears to be one-to-one correspondence between oral sounds and graphic letters.

But the problem appears when we remember that the three-letter sequence <man> doesn't always appear by itself. Consider the word *mane*, for example. Unlike the Scandinavians, who add special letters to the alphabet, or the French and Spanish, who put special markings over some letters, in English we show the change of vowel sound from *man* to *mane* by adding an extra letter as a marker. Our writing system uses this *vowel/consonant/E* pattern to differentiate two sets of English vowels: *pan/pane, can/cane, van/vane*, as well as *hat/hate, mat/mate, rat/rate*, etc.

This simple example already shows that phonics is really a matter of relating orthographic patterns to phonological patterns, not individual letters to individual sounds. In order to know the value of the <a>, we need to recognize that the <e> is there before we get to the <n>; so we can't simply identify the letters from left to right. We have to jump around to see the pattern as a whole, not just the series of letters.

Our <man> allows for a very consistent shift when <e> is added at the end, but let's go further. *Main* and *Maine* sound the same as *mane*. Not only English, but all alphabetically written languages have *homophones,* words that mean different things but sound the same. Another spelling pattern is found in *man/main, pan/pain.* Adding <i> to the <a> is perhaps helpful for readers, since words like *mane, main* and *Maine* look different even though they sound the same.

But what about *manic* and *maniac*? In *manic* the /a/ is the same as in *man,* but in *maniac* it's the long vowel of *mane.* Another pattern.

None of what I've discussed so far is capricious. Everything is patterned. However, the patterns aren't simple — and they don't follow a one-letter-one-sound rule. The phonic relationships in spelling aren't that easy.

The roots of spelling

These and other English spelling patterns reflect the history of the language. English has more complexities than other languages because of the multiple language roots that contributed to it.

The letter <n>, for example, seems to be a stable spelling of /n/, as in the last sound in *man.* But /n/ can also be represented in other spellings:

➤ From our Anglo-Saxon and Danish roots we use <kn> as in *know, knew, knee, knight, knife,* etc.

➤ From Greek or Old English and German we have words starting with <gn>, as in *gnaw, gnat, gneiss.* (But watch out for *ignite, igneous, ignore,* etc.)

➤ From Greek also comes the <pn> spelling in *pneumonia* and *pneumatic.*

➤ From French roots come <gn> words like *campaign, reign* and *sign, resign, design.* (But notice that when we add a suffix to *sign* to make it *signal,* the <g> and <n> represent separate sounds. That happens also with *designate.* But if the affixes are grammatical like *s, ed* or *ing,* there is no /g/: *signs, signed, signing.* Pretty complicated, but still patterned!)

➤ Another problem for spelling /n/ occurs when it becomes what linguists call "nasal." In many dialects, /n/ all but disappears up the nose before certain consonants, particularly /t/ and /d/, as in *want, went, band, bend.* The spelling keeps the <n> even though the sound is hardly heard.

You thought that <n> was a nice dependable letter for spelling /n/, and now I've made it too damn complicated for words, right? *Damn*? Where did the /n/ go in *damn* (also *damns, damned, damning*)? Never mind, it comes back in *damnation* and *damnable.*

And lest you think this is the work of the devil, notice that *hymn* seems to work that way too — in *hymnal,* that is, though not in *hymns.* These changes aren't the result of any silent-letter rule; they are simply attempts to retain the spelling even though the sound appears only with derivational endings. *Bomb* works the same way. A final /b/ is heard in *bombard* and *bombastic* but not in *bombing, bombs* and *bombed*. Keeping the spelling consistent is useful for grammatical functions because it helps readers and writers recognize the meaning relationships between related words.

What does all this prove? Simply that language is complex, not simple. Meaning, grammar and etymology, as well as the representation of the sound system, contribute to the spelling of particular words and patterns of words. "Simplifying" English spelling would add a whole new set of problems to this complexity.

Homographs

Just as different words may share the same sound (homophones), they may also share the same spelling (homographs). *Read/read, lead/lead* and *desert/desert* are examples. Some homographs may be related in their meaning as *read/read* or *desert/desert* are (but not *dessert*). Some have no meaning relationship and usually have different origins or histories, like *lead/lead*. The word "homonym" is sometimes mistakenly used as the equivalent of either homophone or homograph, but homonym actually refers to words that both look and sound alike. *Bear, beat, base, cape, fawn, hamper, will, right, left* are a few of the many homonyms in English.

Conventional spelling

If only phonics had been used, no standardized system of English spelling would ever have been possible.

William Shakespeare signed his will with two different spellings of his name, and no one thought anything of it because, at the time, the notion of a single, legal, standard spelling wasn't yet established. The Oxford dictionary lists these early spellings for *cat*: *catt, catte, kat, katt, katte*, all current into the 17th century. Works in Middle English by authors like Chaucer were translated into the spellings of other English dialects so they could be read more broadly. (Cummings, 1988, p. 21)

Since each dialect invented spellings according to how the words sounded in that dialect, if only phonics had been used, no standardized system of English spelling would ever have developed. Two other principles, neither directly relating to phonics, became important in producing common spellings across dialects:

> ➤ The semantic principle — words with related meanings should be spelled similarly: *sign, signal, design* and *designate* all keep the <gn> spelling. That's a help to both readers and writers.

➤ The etymological principle — spellings should reflect the derivation of the words: *knee, know, knife* show their Germanic origins. Some English words have kept the spellings of the original language: *chef, chauffeur, chateau* from French, for example. Others have pseudo-derivational spellings: *scissors, scythe* and *rescind* were all assumed to derive from the Latin word *scindere* (to cut), although only the latter actually does (Cummings, p. 18).

Perhaps I should add this one other as well:

➤ The power of tradition — words should look familiar and like other spellings.

English spelling evolved over time, but it wasn't until the 19th century that spelling became fully conventional. "Standard" spellings of words were established and stored in dictionaries at that time, and literate users of English were expected to use these in their writing in a consistent way.

However, there's a circularity here. The dictionary reflects and records use, but doesn't create it. Samuel Johnson, who developed a dictionary in 1775, warned us:

> Those who have been persuaded to think well of my design, will require that it should fix our language, and put a stop to those alterations which time and chance have hitherto been suffered to make in it without opposition. With this consequence I will confess that I flattered myself for a while; but now begin to fear that I have indulged expectation which neither reason nor experience can justify. . . . we laugh at the elixir that promises to prolong life to a thousand years; and with equal justice may the lexicographer be derided, who being able to produce no example of a nation that has preserved their words and phrases from mutability, shall imagine that his dictionary can embalm his language, and secure it from corruption and decay . . .

Dictionaries can record the language but can't prevent it from changing afterwards. And even though we can pick out common spelling principles, standard spellings are often quite arbitrary, established by a consensus among lexicographers, printers, writers and publishers. I don't mean that they met and agreed, just that they worked at being consistent with each other.

American spelling conventions come closest to actually being invented by committee. Noah Webster was part of a group of American intellectuals intent on separating American literature from British. Different American spellings would help to accomplish that, they believed. But Webster wasn't only a maker of dictionaries. He also wrote the most influential and important elementary school textbook of his time. Popularly known as the *Blue-backed Speller*, it was more than just a spelling book. Webster believed that children should learn to spell a core vocabulary of words before learning to read and write. His pupils memorized word spellings and spelled out new words as they met them in their reading. Virtually every American child who learned to read and write in the middle of the 19th century had to start by learning Webster's spellings.

Apart from standardizing American spelling, his method probably contributed to the notion that words should be pronounced according to how they are spelled. What a peculiar reverse application of phonics! We first standardize spellings to avoid the variations that different dialect pronunciations produce, and then we began to tell kids they should change their pronunciations to match these spellings!

Of course there's nothing intrinsically superior about American or British spelling. Nor is conventional spelling necessary to successful reading and writing. Many fine writers would be early dropouts from a spelling competition. And readers easily cope with variations in spelling to make sense of their reading.

There are clear advantages to having conventional spellings, however. Besides making printers, typists and editors more consistent with each other, conventional spelling probably facilitates written communication within the very large international communities that share English, French, Spanish and other widely used languages as their languages of literacy. Moreover, being conventional in spelling contributes to a sense of consistency and orderliness in written language.

A basic contradiction

Ironically, the decisions societies make to conventionalize spelling make it impossible to achieve anything like a one-letter-to-one-sound correspondence! Let me describe the basic contradiction.

Linguists tell us that all languages are rule governed, particularly the phonology, morphology and grammar. Learning language to the point of conventionality means internalizing the socially agreed upon rules and being able to count on them to work in producing and comprehending language. (Don't confuse language conventions with school rules, however. In school we may teach that there's no double negative, but society teaches that there is, in some dialects: "No, Ma'am, I didn't use no double negative.")

So how does the decision to make spelling conventional contradict the premise that language is rule governed? Here are three ways:

> ➤ It establishes standard spellings across dialects that don't share a single phonological rule system.

➤ It requires choices: keep the spelling of words with related meanings consistant *or* follow the morphophonemic shifts in sounds and have very different spellings for closely related words (so *sign, signify, design* and *designate* would become *sine, signify, dezine* and *dezignate*).

➤ It doesn't allow a consistent matching of the features of two-dimensional space that spelling requires with the time sequence that speech uses.

Let's look at each of those issues in a bit more detail.

Dialect differences

If we agree on a single spelling, we necessarily disagree on how that spelling relates to the sounds.

In my dialect, *bog, cog, dog, fog, frog, grog, hog, jog, log, smog, tog* divide into two rhyming groups, depending on the vowel sound. The first list is *bog, cog, grog, jog, smog, tog,* the second *dog, fog, frog, hog, and log.* But in every North American dialect of English those lists will be somewhat different; in fact, some people will use the same vowel sound for all. Yet all groups use the same <og> spelling for all of the words, and I say it again: if we agree on a single spelling, we are disagreeing on how that spelling relates to the sounds of English, and some or most of us are bound to be violating the one-sound-one-spelling rule.

Help in my midwestern dialect has a distinct /l/. In Louisiana it's likely to be *he'p,* and in Oklahoma it's *hey-ulp* with two syllables. Again we use a common spelling. If we were to establish a phonics/spelling rule and all use it consistently, we would be inventing spellings that might be logical, but certainly not conventional. (We'll talk later about how kids do invent unconventional but rule-governed spellings as they learn to spell.)

None of these dialect speech differences is right or wrong. All languages are really families of dialects, more or less mutually understandable, that differ from each other in phonology, vocabulary, grammar and other ways. If spelling is standardized across dialects — as it is in English and most other languages — phonic "rules" will vary and be inconsistent from dialect to dialect. My *media* has no /r/ at the end, but my *meteor* does. On the other hand, someone from Maine may have an /r/ on *media* but not on *meteor*, depending on whether the following word starts with a vowel or a consonant.

On the next page is a diagram that illustrates the logic of phonics relationships across dialects. By convention, spellings are constant, phonology is variable: words are pronounced differently in different dialects. So phonics, the relationship between constant spelling and variable phonology, must also be variable. There is no *single phonics* that applies to all readers; phonics will be different for each dialect of a language.

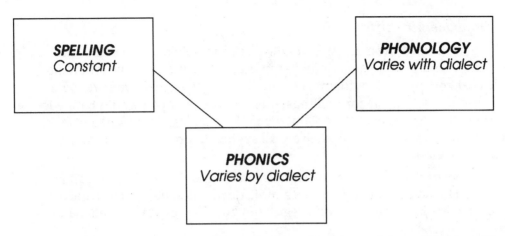

Furthermore, since all language changes over time while standard spellings are held constant by conventional agreement, the phonic relationships will also change. Even the close matches between spelling and sound patterns in some dialects will begin to diverge. For example, the <gh> in *right, light* and *night* corresponds to a sound found only in some Scottish dialects of English.

Schwa

It would be too confusing if words had two spellings depending on whether or not they were stressed.

The special case of schwa is an example of language change over time, and it cuts across English dialects. Around the 14th century in England, all unaccented vowels shifted to a common vowel, usually called *schwa* and represented by linguists as /ə/. This presents the spelling system with a dilemma. Should we spell the same word in two different ways depending on whether the vowel is stressed or unstressed, or should the spelling always be the stressed form?

The system chose the latter option — for example, we spell *man* the same in "I am a man" and in "My name is Goodman," even though the vowel changes to schwa in the unstressed syllable. And because function words, which are among the most common, are usually unstressed, that choice has a significant impact on our use of the schwa. "Can I go to the store?" has unstressed vowels in *can*, which is pronounced /kin/, and *to*, which becomes /ti/ or even /t/. But notice that in the answer, "Yes, you can," the vowel in *can* is stressed. The noun *can*, as in *a tin can*, can only have a stressed vowel.

You'd think that young readers would be mightily confused by the fact that schwa can be represented by any vowel in spelling patterns, but there's nothing in the research to support that suspicion. And just think how confusing it would be if words had two spellings depending on whether or not they were stressed!

Morphophonemic shifts

I've mentioned the changes that take place in phonemes when they are followed by certain other sounds, either in the same word or in the following word. That, too, presents a dilemma for the spelling system. If we stick to the one-sound-one-letter rule for spellings, *situation*, for example, would be spelled something like <sitchyooayshun>. But we prefer *education* to look like *educate*. *Please/pleasure, rate/ration, fact/factual* are all spelled to preserve the meaning/ derivational relationships.

Past tense affixes provide an example of changes that could bring all kinds of trouble. However, although from a simplistic phonics view such changes look confusingly irregular, they are very regular in how the spelling system handles them.

In English, the most common indication of past tense involves adding an ending to the verb. There are three forms of the past tense ending in speech, depending on the last sound of the verb's base form:

➤ *Wanted* and *waded* take a /ɨd/ form. (The "barred i" vowel is very short and comes close to the schwa in sound.)

➤ *Grabbed, lagged, barred, roamed, groaned, paced, mailed, amazed, saved* take a /d/ form.

➤ *Walked, stepped, passed* take a /t/.

But all three forms generally use <ed> for the spelling. The British also use <t> spellings, as in *spilt*. We prefer *spilled*, but we do use some <t> endings, as in *slept* and *kept*. Actually, there's no reason these words couldn't use the regular <ed> ending, since readers would have a hard time saying the past tense any differently anyway.

Adding <s> to verbs and nouns results in similar variations: /s/ in *drops, ticks, pots*; /z/ in *robs, beds, eggs* and /ɨz/ in *mazes, boxes, glasses*. But we use <s> or <es> in all the spellings, regardless of which sound is used in oral language. Here, too, the decision was made to be consistent in keeping related words looking alike. As always, there are exceptions, of course: *life/lives* and *knife/knives*, for example.

Two letters for one sound

Some other spelling dilemmas have to do with the differences in how the two systems, orthography and phonology, must work. As I said before, each language that uses the Roman alphabet has had to make some accommodations to it to fit the phonology of that language.

English has two different but related phonemes that we usually represent with the same combination of letters, <th>: the sound in *this* and the sound in *thin*. The Greek alphabet had letters for these sounds (Θ and δ), but the Roman alphabet didn't. Nor do they occur in most European languages. So we use <th> to represent both. Similarly, <ch> or <tch> represents the single phoneme /č/, and <sh> represents /š/. Again you might think these accomodations would cause real problems: won't some readers treat the <th> as separate letters and read *father* as *fat-her*? But as miscue research has demonstrated, readers aren't often fooled by these digraphs (letter pairs), because they use the context to predict whether one sound or two are represented.

Pattern markers

What has often been called the "silent e" in English spellings is actually a pattern marker, as I demonstrated earlier. Here are two groups of words spelled the same except for the final <e>: *rat/rate, rot/rote, rip/ripe, cur/cure, her/here*. In each case the final <e> marks which of two vowels is represented.

An <e> is also used to mark other patterns. Short words ending in vowels (except for function words) add <e> as a marker: *doe, tie, rye, due, see*. As spellings became standardized, apparently printers worried that words with only two letters might get lost or be mistaken for function words, so they added a third letter. We also don't like English words to end in <v>, so we stick an <e> after it: *love, have, give, groove*.

This vowel/consonant/e pattern affects some other spelling as well. The reason that consonants are sometimes doubled before <ed> and <er> endings is to avoid any confusion with that pattern. So we have *diner/dinner, super/supper, later/latter, coned/conned, robed/robbed, stared/starred*.

Summary

Recent works have given us good insights into how English spelling works (Wilde, 1992; Cummings, 1985; Read, 1986), and I could say a lot more on the intricacies of it. All I want to make clear, however, is that no simple reform would solve all the problems of English spelling — and it might create as many problems as it solved. We could eliminate alternate spellings for homophones like *meat/meet/mete*, for example, but in doing so we would turn them into homonyms that look and sound alike. And besides, as phonology changed over time, any reformed spelling would soon need more reforming.

But my best argument against spelling reform is that we don't need it. Readers are not hampered by English spelling complexity. In the next section I'll try to make clear why that is so, by examining how we use phonics and spelling in our reading and writing.

5

*To
standardize
spellings we must
sacrifice the consistency
of the phonics rules for
the consistency of
spelling.*

Phonics: the connector

After looking carefully at phonology and orthography, I now want to bring together what is known about phonics, the third graphophonics system and the one that connects the first two.

A key misconception

Here is a key misconception in understanding the importance of phonics to reading and writing, and its converse:

➤ If I know how to say something and I know phonics, I will be able to write the same thing with accurate spelling.

➤ If I see print and I know phonics, I will be able to sound it out and then understand what it says.

The first statement refers to spelling. For the moment, let's set aside the very important difference between spelling and writing and just examine this key question: is there a straightforward set of phonics rules that will generate the spellings of English words from their sounds?

When linguists first became seriously interested in reading, about 25 years ago, several studies were done to see if computers could generate spellings by using rules based on the sounds of the words, and vice-versa (Hanna et al., 1966; Cronnell, 1971; Weir and Venezky, 1968; and later, others). Here is my own, admittedly simplified, summary of the findings:

If we were to establish a sequence of rules the computer had to apply *in order*, then the computer would be fairly accurate (90% or so). The rules would have to go from the least general and smallest group of words to the largest or residual group. We would program the computer by telling it: "First check to see if it's one of this set of words. If it is, then spell it _____. If not, look for this pattern. If it is, spell it _____ . . ." and so on until we got to: "For all others, use _____."

For instance, let's take words with a /š/ sound. First we'll need to tell the computer that there are a small set of words that spell that sound with <ch>, specifically *chef, chauffeur, chateau*, etc. (It won't help the computer to know that these are French borrowings.)

Next, we'll start with limited and minor rules. For instance, we'll need to alert the computer that:

➤ In words that include the affixes <tion> (*condition*) or <tial> (*initial*), the sound seems to be spelled with a <t>. (Note that here, as in many cases, the computer must look for and recognize a morphophonemic pattern — it certainly won't succeed by looking at letters one at a time or by listening to sounds one at a time.)

➤ Some words need to relate: *face* and *race* become *facial* and *racial*.

➤ There is a minor rule for spelling /š/ with <s> when it's followed by <u>, as in *sure, sugar, insure, assure*. (Words like *sum, Sunday* and *insult* don't fit this rule, but it's still a rule because the <u> in words like *sure* has a /yu/ sound.)

➤ There's a group of words that spell /š/ with <ss>: *tissue, Russia, pressure*.

Finally, when we've exhausted all the minor rules, in order, we can instruct the computer: in all other cases try <sh> . . . And then start the same process all over again for each English dialect!

Actually, the studies are pretty interesting if you like that sort of thing. But I'm going to stop here and return to the basic misconception: that phonics can produce standard spellings in writing and accurate word recognition in reading.

What the studies discovered in that connection is that using all the spelling rules available can at best give someone a set of alternatives to choose from within a particular context. If we want the rules to generate 100% standard spellings, they fall far short of the mark. And that doesn't even take into consideration dialect variations in phonology — the studies didn't even consider dialects. But it's precisely because spelling is standardized across dialects that the rules of phonics aren't like other language rules. We sacrifice the consistency of rules for the consistency of spelling.

Now let's go back and also remember that spelling and writing are not the same thing. Spelling rules don't produce punctuation and don't determine word boundaries. Is it *all right*, or *alright*? *A way* or *away*? Is it *cup cake* or *cup-cake* or *cupcake*? And more importantly, writing isn't just spelling words correctly. How can I write if I'm limited to just those words I'm sure I can spell correctly and my rules only get me close?

Now the corollary: can I read by "sounding out" words? Again the answer is that phonics can only put me in the neighborhood. Even if I sounded out every letter in sequence, I wouldn't come close, because there's no one-to-one correspondence and because sounds change with the context, as we've seen repeatedly. Still, phonics does get us into the "neighborhood" and that may be good enough, because then other syntactic and semantic information can fill in and help us get to the sense we're seeking.

Our miscue research revealed what readers do when they don't recognize a word in the text they're reading: they work around different possibilities to see if anything might sound right. Incidentally, more confident readers are less likely to produce multiple attempts at a given text word. They seem to expect that important words will come up again in the text (and if they don't, they can't be that important), and they don't waste effort on "getting" all the words as they read. Less confident readers, particularly (in our studies) older students in grades 8 and 10, produce many unsuccessful attempts to sound out every "new" word. By the time they give up, they've lost any meaning they were building.

So what's the use of phonics?

All readers can and do use phonics within the complex process of making sense of print as they read and saying what they want to say as they write.

Perhaps a lot of you reading this think you're on to my game. I've built an overwhelming case to argue that phonics doesn't work, that it's far too complicated to be of any use in reading and writing. But if that's what you think, think again. All readers (at least those who can hear) can and do use phonics. But they use it within the complex process of making sense of print as they read, and of expressing comprehensibly what they need to say as they write. And it's most useful when it's used in just the right amount: not too much, not too litle. "A little dab'll do ya", Leland Jacobs used to say, appropriating a commercial jingle.

Here is the heart of my argument: children equip themselves best for reading and writing by building *a personal understanding of the phonics of their own forms of English*, rules for relating their own phonology to print. They'll know that those rules aren't as dependable as other language rules because standard spellings are arbitrary — neither capricious nor random, but the result of human social decisions and agreements. And they'll know that's okay, because they have lots of other information to use.

For those who can hear and who know oral language, phonics is an important component of reading alphabetically written language. But it is only one component, and it has predictable values only in meaningful context.

How do you say *going to*? Try it in: "I'm *going to* the store." And now try it in: "I'm *going to* go home now." Most of us say something like *gonna* in the second case. But we can't say it that way in the first sentence — the pronunciation is different because the words have different grammatical functions in the two sentences. We don't know how to pronounce the words until we decide what their grammar is.

Sometimes spelling accounts for these changes: *don't* for *do not*, should've for *should have*. But more often, as in *going to*, the spelling stays the same. We say *with'm* for both *with him* and *with them*.

Phonics is always both personal and social, because we must build relationships between our own personal speech (our idiolect), the speech of our community (our dialect) and the social conventions of writing. It is always contextual because the values of both sound and letter patterns change in the phonological, grammatical and meaning contexts they occur in. And it's never more than part of the process of reading and writing.

For all these reasons, phonics is learned best *in the course of* learning to read and write, *not as a prerequisite*. In fact, our phonics is determined by our speaking, listening, reading and writing *experiences*!

Phonics in reading

This is a book on phonics, not on reading and writing. But to understand the value of phonics in reading and writing I must set it in those processes.

As you read this section, keep in mind a simple, easily verified fact: even average readers read silently far faster than they talk or read orally. If we were producing an internal match for the sounds of each word, we could not be reading so fast. So, reading silently must involve getting to the meaning of the passage we are reading using less than all the information available to us. To put phonics in its proper place, we need to understand how we do that.

Reading is not the accurate sequential recognition of words. I don't usually start with a negative statement in defining reading, but I will in this case because any misunderstanding of the role of phonics in reading comes partly from thinking that each and every word in a text must be accurately recognized before we can make sense of it. That's not true. If it were true, reading would have developed a phonics that would work best on isolated words and that readers would have to modify in context. Remember that all unaccented vowels are schwa, so virtually every function word sounds different on a list than in context: *to, and, for*, etc. And in polysyllabic words the same vowels have different pronunciation in stressed and unstressed syllables.

Please read this sequence rapidly out loud:

He's going to climb and climb to the top of the roof to get the ball. I'm going with him.

Now read this list of words:

and, ball, climb, get, going, he's, him, I'm, of, roof, the, to, top, with

In reading the text sequence you probably read something like: *He's gonna climb 'n climb t' th' top o' th' roof t' git th' ball. I'm goin' with 'm.* Identifying each word separately would be like reading a list of words rather than a story or text. In fact, you can tell when readers are trying to identify separate words, because they give each word the same intonation — they sound as if they're reading lists. Readers can't sound out words letter by letter, nor can they make sense of written language by accurately identifying each word. Fortunately, neither is necessary for effective and efficient reading.

Miscue analysis research

I suspected that words were harder to read in lists than in real stories when I first started studying reading. Many teachers understood that even then, but I took the opportunity of my first miscue studies to check it out with a large group of first, second and third graders. Before they read a story, I had them read a list of words they would be seeing in it. It turned out that even first graders could read, in the stories, two out of three of the words they couldn't recognize on the lists. For the third graders it was four out of five. I randomly chose half of all the children in one school to make sure I had a full range of abilities — some first graders were reading well above their grade and some third graders well below. The reading material I used for the group as a whole ranged from pre-primer to eighth grade. In all cases, they read far more words in the story contexts than they did in isolation (Goodman, 1965).

What could explain this? I've spent a good part of my life finding out. I've studied the reading miscues of hundreds of kids at all levels of ability. The heart of what I learned is this: *reading is making sense of print, and that's a much more efficient process than accurately identifying words.*

In the context of a story or a piece of expository text, readers focus on getting to the meaning. If they encounter unfamiliar words, these words occur in grammatical patterns that determine their syntactic function (the part of speech they represent). As the reader builds meaning, predictions are made and inferences drawn about what to expect. So, when reading in context readers often guess the meaning and even the identity of unfamiliar words. Alongside the syntactic, semantic and pragmatic information readers use, a little bit of phonics goes a long way. It's enough to confirm a prediction or choose between possible alternatives. For *They went into the* ____. the reader predicts *house* because the characters were on their way home from school. And sure enough, there's the <h> in *house*.

I also learned that readers have not just one but three systems of information to bring to any text — graphophonic, syntactic and semantic — and that each one supports the other two. In the course of making sense of print, we use all three systems, and in using them we learn them. We learn what *house* looks like when we encounter it, and later we might learn that *honest* and *hour* are spelled with <h> too, although they don't have the /h/ sound.

If learners are learning to write while they're learning to read, they will learn how words are spelled as they read. They'll be "reading like writers," as Frank Smith (1982) puts it. They'll note words they see in their reading that they remember trying to spell in their writing. They'll also build an ability to deal with a range of different fonts and allographs.

Early in my work I called reading a "psycholinguistic guessing game," to emphasize the important roles that prediction and inference play in reading. Readers have a lot of information from each of the three systems, but they use just enough from each to make sense of the text. As they read they learn to read.

Let's look at some examples from my research. They clearly show readers of different abilities engaged in the guessing game, and reveal how those readers use phonics in relation to the other cue systems.

Below is a sample of a beginner reading a pre-primer "story" called "Look Here," from a controlled vocabulary basal that was unfamiliar to him. According to the teacher's manual, he would have been taught phonics, and would also be introduced to each "new" word. The pictures reveal that Pepper is a dog and the children, Jimmy and Sue, have put him in a wagon.

Come, Pepper and Sue.

an'
Come and (ride.)

The reader doesn't sound out the words. He starts to read them as if they were words on a list: "Come, Pepper, and, Sue, Come, an'." Then he pauses briefly and says nothing for "ride."

(Ride) Pepper.

(Ride) Sue.

           an'

(Ride) Pepper and Sue

On page 2 he skips "Ride" on each line without hesitating. But as he gets to the third line he reads "Pepper an' Sue" with a more natural intonation, making it sound like a phrase and end like a sentence. He reduces "and" more naturally, losing the final consonant. However, the vowel is still not reduced to a schwa or lost altogether as we would normally read such phrases, as in "bread 'n butter."

Look here.

Here we come.

Look at Pepper.

Look at Sue.

There are no miscues on page 3. He starts as if the words were on a list, but ends reading "Look at Pepper, Look at Sue" like a story, with appropriate intonation.

      is

Here we go, Jimmy and Sue.

Here we go, Pepper.

Run

Ride, Jimmy and Sue.

Run   *run*

Ride, Pepper, ride.

On the final page he substitutes "is" for "we" on the first line, though he read "we" correctly earlier and reads it correctly in the line below. Finally, he substitutes "run" for "ride" three times.

Explanation

I suspect the reader decided at the begining that *ride* was a new word. Readers with similar school experiences often looked up as they read for us and said, "We haven't had that word yet." Clearly they didn't feel responsible for reading words they hadn't been introduced to.

My hunch is confirmed on page 2, where he seems to have decided deliberately to skip *ride* each time it occurs. I did a study of omissions in my miscue data and concluded that it can be a deliberate strategy readers use with unfamiliar words — not so much with words they don't know as with words they're not sure they know.

Even with this stiff little "story" we get a sense from his intonation by the bottom of page 2 that he's trying to make some sense of what he's reading. Page 3 confirms that, not because there are no miscues but because of the more natural intonation at the end.

On page 4 two important things happen. First is his unusual substitution of *is* for *we*. This certainly doesn't advance his understanding of the text, particularly since he doesn't correct. But it shows that he's no longer just saying words in a list. His experience with the pre-primer texts he's used to reading leads him to predict *is* after *Here,* even though it doesn't look or sound like *we.* He's learned to expect *is* to follow *here* at the start of a sentence.

Why did he substitute *run* for *ride*? Both start with <r> and /r/ (letter and sound); both are verbs; both make sense. In fact, what may have bothered him at the beginning of the story is that *ride* is being used as an imperative, while in real language it's seldom used without an object. His *run* is a more appropriate verb for this context.

This reader shows that he's using all three cue systems to try to make sense of what he's reading. Is he doing so proficiently? Not yet. But the unnatural text doesn't help much.

In the next example, Janice is reading a more advanced first grade basal story called "Two New Hats."

One morning old Mrs. Duck said,
Mr.

"What a good day for a walk!

I will take a walk in the park."

And away she went.

___

Janice's first two miscues are on "Mrs.," which she reads as "Mr." on the first line, and "Miss" on the next page, which she corrects.

After a time Mrs. Duck saw
© *Miss*

a big old apple tree.

"I will go over there," she said.
© *the*

"I will walk un / der the apple tree."

___

Two lines later she reads "there" as "the" but also corrects this miscue. In the last sentence on the page she reads "under" with an exaggerated separation between the syllables.

Something came out of the tree.
© *k: –*

But Mrs. Duck did not see it.

"Oh! Oh!", said Mrs. Duck.

"Something came down!" →

She has what we call a partial on "came" at the top of the next page. She says /k/ and then says the word as expected. Later she reads "Something came down . . ." as if she expects it to continue but then leaves it hanging and goes on to the next paragraph.

lookeded
Mrs. Duck looked here and there.

But she did not see a thing^

Under
under the (old) apple tree.

A. © the
And |on she went for a walk.

In the next line she substitutes "lookeded" for "looked." Farther along she reads "But she did not see a thing" as if it were a finished sentence. Then she starts "under" as if it begins a new sentence. Now she omits "old." Finally, in the last line she has another partial on "And" and reads "the" for "she," which she corrects.

Explanation

Mrs. is a written language abbreviation for a word lost from most dialects of English (Appalachian speakers say *Mizrus*, not *Missus*). You can't "sound out" *Mrs.* any more than you can sound out *Mr.* The text doesn't provide any clue to gender, so Janice substitutes *Mr.* But then the text says *she*, so Janice tries *Miss* but this time corrects, probably because the word just doesn't look like that. (This may seem like a simple issue but such miscues are common even among fifth and sixth graders. The issue is not just one of phonics but of concepts: who is called Mr., Mrs., Miss? And which abbreviation stands for which oral term?)

There are three points in this text where Janice's predictions are misled by unusual syntax, all involving prepositional phrases:

➤ *I will go over there* she reads as, *I will go over the . . .* Her experience leads her to expect a noun phrase to follow *over,* so she reads *the,* using visual information also emanating from *there.* The *she said* that follows doesn't fit her prediction, so she reprocesses, possibly even taking a second look, and corrects herself.

➤ She reads *Something came down . . .* as if she again expects a noun phrase to follow *down.* How do we know that? Her intonation rises and then hangs there. She doesn't correct this time. She hasn't miscued on any words here, but she hasn't produced an acceptable reading either, since she's left herself with an unfinished sentence. So I suspect she may be a bit confused about the meaning.

➤ At the end she reads *And on she* as *And on the . . .* Again the text misleads her; she expects *on* to be a preposition followed by an object. *She* and *the* look a lot alike, so she gets initial confirmation of her prediction. But what follows disconfirms. This time she corrects.

It's obvious that simple reliance on phonics can't solve Janice's problems with these unusual syntactic patterns. In controlling the words in this "story," the authors and editors have created clumsy, unpredictable grammar. Her miscues show her trying to find a structure that will allow her to make sense of the reading. The text certainly has contributed to her miscues, as it would for many readers.

Over-correction, as in *lookeded*, is very common among young readers. When words end in /k/ they take the /d/ form of the past tense morpheme. But when they end in /d/ they take the /ɪd/ form. The confusion is not one of phonics. It's an issue of whether the base form is *look* or *looked*. The word most commonly confused like this is *drowned* — many children produce *drownded* orally. Speakers of Black English, Pidgin and other dialects that tend not to use past tense affixes are more likely to add these extra endings, perhaps because teachers have convinced them that they're prone to omit endings.

Ending her sentence after *thing* is a common miscue for readers just moving into texts where sentences are longer than lines. Basal publishers think that by keeping sentences one line long they're making the texts easier. Actually, all they're doing is building an unnatural one-sentence-one-line expectation.

Janice's omission of *old* reveals the folly of unnatural repetition in controlled vocabulary texts. We need information like the age of the tree only once (I call it the "rule of economy"), so the second reference she reads as just *the apple tree*. She doesn't expect *old* the third time either, and omits it.

From these two representative readers it's clear that even beginning readers use phonics, but only in the context of trying to make sense of the texts they are reading. Even with these rather unnatural basal texts, they still aren't simply sounding out each word. These readers already know that just concentrating on getting the words right won't get them to the meaning.

But what happens if a child is taught to over-rely on phonics and diligently tries to sound out each word? Patricia, a second grade African-American child is reading a children's book reprinted in a basal. It's a picture book, so no page has a lot of print. Each chunk below represents a page:

        © *lef'*   *valley*   *tender*
One day a man|left his village to tend to his

1. *fl- for/*2. *flower*   *foun'* *oh*
field of corn. But he found only an open

places   *your*   *str-*
place where young corn had stood straight

    all
and tall.

Patricia starts out her reading preoccupied with getting the words right. She says "lef'" for "left," which in her rural Mississippi dialect sounds right to her. But she corrects it. Perhaps her teacher has been admonishing Patricia and her classmates to say the final <t> and <d>. Next, she substitutes "valley" for "village," "tender" *for "tend" and "flower" for "field." These real-word substitutions keep their grammatical functions but don't quite make sense, and none are corrected. She says "foun'" for "found," not correcting, corrects "places" for "place" but not "oh" for "only." At the end of the first page she reads "your corn had stood straight and all" with appropriate intonation and without correction, since that's a phrase that makes sense to her.*

door $barken

The man looked down at the poor broken

$sta-ul-ks   low   dozin'

stalks and a saw a large turtle dozing in

the sun. He picked up the turtle and

carried him back to the village.

She seems to be trying to do two things: get the words right (sound them out) and make sense of the story. But she can't do both, so she swings from one way of reading to the other. On this page she reads "poor" as "door": they look very similar but don't rhyme. She reads the next two words as "$barken $sta-ul-ks" ($ identifies non-words), saying each sound but not producing sense. She doesn't correct, but then reads the rest of the page with good intonation, saying "low" for "large." She reads "village" this time as if it were a familiar, easily predictable word. Here's her split personality at work. She starts reading, comes to a phrase she decides to use phonics on, settles for phonic nonsense, and then proceeds to make sense of the rest of the page, even getting "village" right although it's not easy to sound out.

wif

The man said, "What can we do to this

He

turtle? He's crushed my corn.

sound $prushish

The people said, "We should punish him.

That   the   sound

That's what we should do."

the $prushes

The man said, "How can we punish him?"

The people said, "Cook him for stew!

She continues in her meaning-getting mode on the next two lines, reading comfortably in her own dialect: "wif" (with) for "to" and "he" for "he's." She reads "sound" for "should" — try sounding out "should"! This story contains a repetitious pattern: the people are trying to think of bad punishments for the turtle who keeps responding "just don't throw me in the river." Notice how Patricia employs a pattern herself: "$prushish" for "punish"

and "$prushes" for "we punish." And she finishes with a strange but to her dialect meaningful sentence that includes "the sound" for "we should." Although it might seem that she's got "the" and "we" confused, note that she's already read both of *them successfully. She's turned "punish" into a noun by putting "the" in front of it. She reads the last line of the page with no miscues — she's back to sense-making.*

             That   excite
The turtle said, "That's exactly what

    I'll   the
to do! I'd make a tasty turtle stew.

But please, don't throw me into the river!"

        The   incited a friend
The man said, "This turtle isn't afraid

for   ©the $prushes
of fire. How can |we| punish him?

                 the
The people said, "Tie him to a tree!"

She reads "that" for "that's" on the next page, appropriate in her dialect. But when she says "excite" for "exactly" she's using her phonics again and doesn't correct. Then she's back to meaning: "I'll make the tasty turtle stew." And she finishes the paragraph without miscues. In the next two lines she puts together a string of nonsense, all seemingly real words but using phonics and giving up on meaning. She also says "the $prushish" for "we punish"

again, but she corrects "the" to "we." Finally she finishes the page with only a substitution of "the" for "a," showing us by changing an indefinite to a definite noun phrase that she's using syntactic cues.

    Patricia has shown us here that she controls every aspect of the reading process that she needs to make sense of this text. But she's preoccupied with phonics as a strategy and thinks she must use it.

    As the story continues, the "isn't afraid of" pattern recurs several times, but here is what Patricia does in the successive occurrences:

        The   incite 'fraid
The man said, "This turtle isn't afraid of fire.

     is   ropes
This turtle isn't afraid of rope.

The man said, "This turtle isn't afraid of fire.

    incited   ropes
This turtle isn't afraid of rope.

The   incited   from
This turtle isn't afraid of earth.

On the first line she stays with "incite" for "isn't" but gets "afraid." Next she moves to "is afraid" for "isn't afraid." In the next line she gets "isn't afraid" right! Hurrah! Whoops! She's back to "incited" and stays there for the rest of the story. She doesn't trust herself and falls back on her sounded-out attempt.

I feel deeply for Patricia and all those like her. She has all she needs to make sense of print, and does in fact make sense of it at times. The problem is that she doesn't trust herself. She seems to feel safer settling for sounded-out nonsense than her own constructed meaning. That's what phonics as instruction can do to young readers. Very likely, eventually, Patricia will give herself permission to make sense of print as she reads, but she may always feel that somehow she's cheating and that she's not really a good reader.

Efficient and effective reading

Efficiency doesn't just save time and energy — It also prevents readers from bogging down and losing meaning.

These young readers illustrate well how phonics works and ought to work in the reading of an alphabetic language like English. There is no doubt that all readers use phonics, as I've defined it: a set of relationships between the written and oral systems of the language. But to be effective — that is, to make sense of print — readers must use phonic information along with meaning and grammar cues.

Patricia does that when, for instance, she reads *He picked up the turtle and carried him back to the village* with good intonation and without miscues, even though she read *village* as *valley* a page earlier. She relies on phonics alone when she repeatedly miscues on *punish* and *isn't*. And she mistrusts her own meaning construction when she first gets *isn't afraid* right and then abandons it.

Effective reading is making sense of print, but efficiency is also important. Efficiency is being effective with the least possible amount of energy and effort, and the fewest cues. Efficiency doesn't just save time and energy — it prevents bogging down and losing meaning. Patricia is trying to do what I suspect she's been taught: read carefully, look at all the letters, don't guess. That strategy produces *door $barken $sta-ul-ks* for *poor broken stalks*. She's using so much phonic information that she's overloading herself and losing meaning altogether.

I suspect this rural child knows what corn stalks are, but she doesn't give herself permission to use what she knows. She uses too much of the phonic information and too little of the meaning and language structure. So she's not only ineffective in getting to the meaning, but she's also inefficient. Efficiency requires that she sample just enough of the phonic information to make predictions and inferences, as well as confirm her prior expectations of the text.

I suppose one could argue that if she were even more careful she would never say *door* for *poor*. But *poor* is used in an unusual sense here. Since Patricia can't figure out what the sense of *poor* is, she picks *door*, which is very similar in appearance. That's a reasonably good phonics strategy, but she doesn't test her word to fit either the meaning here or the grammatical position, a noun modifier. She gives up on meaning and produces phonic nonsense for the next two words. She isn't using phonics as one information source among several. She's using it as if it's the only one that's safe to use. That's both inefficient and ineffective.

Yet she *can* be so efficient that she seems to be exerting no effort at all: *The man said, What can we do wif this turtle? He crushed my corn.* Her rural Mississippi dialect shines through as she reads this, shifting from *to* to her pronunciation of *with*.

Phonics in writing

The story below was written at home by eight-year-old Shoshana for her great-aunt who was terminally ill from cancer. She wrote it spontaneously and without adult input, choosing a folktale form to solve the problem of mortality for herself and her loved one.

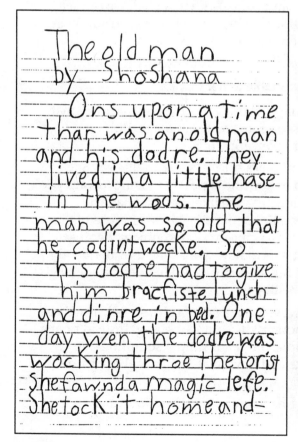

The old man
by Shoshana
   Ons upon a time
thar was an old man
and his dodre. They
lived in a little hase
in the wods. The
man was so old that
he codint wocke. So
his dodre had to give
him bracfiste lunch
and dinre in bed. One
day wen the dodre was
wocking throe the forist
She fawnd a magic lefe.
She tock it home and

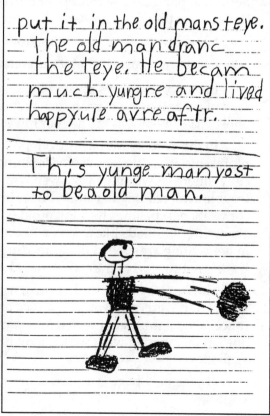

put it in the old mans teye.
The old man dranc
the teye. He becam
much yungre and lived
happy ule avre aftr.

This yunge man yost
to be a old man.

As in many such stories, a pure and simple young person uses magic to solve the problem. Shoshana shows good control of this genre. Her story begins with *Ons upon a time* and ends with the old man, now *much yungre*, living forever, that is, *happyule avre aftr*. Her story has a beginning, a middle and an end. It has a clearly stated problem, an appropriate setting (*a little hase in the wods*), a climax and a solution to the problem. She prefers a female protagonist.

Inventions and conventions

Though she uses non-conventional spellings, Shoshana shows considerable control of spelling and punctuation conventions. She uses periods conventionally at the end of each of her sometimes complex sentences — although she doesn't seem to be into commas yet, at least not for this piece — and she hasn't used the apostrophe in *codint* (couldn't). In comparison with those written by children of similar age and experience, her story is well formed and her control of punctuation is good.

When we divide her spellings into conventional and invented, we can see her use of phonics. The concept of invention is an important one, particularly in the study of phonics. Shoshana's inventions show two forces at play:

➤ her ability to invent a spelling for words she wants to use in the story;

➤ her drive to make her story understandable to her readers.

Invention is always present in language learning; it's the creative force that each of us, and every human society, possesses to create language. But Shoshana's inventions are neither random nor capricious.

In this piece we see her developing phonics rules at work in the way she represents, in writing, how words sound to her. She is clearly moving toward conventions — we know very well which words she intended and have no trouble at all reading her story. She is inventing, but using her awareness of the conventional spellings that surround her in a print-rich environment. Because she writes, she reads like a writer: she attends to how words she uses frequently in her writing are spelled in her reading. But she's not afraid to invent a spelling if she's not sure what the conventional spelling is.

Shoshana's phonics is her own, however, not a set of rules she's learned at school. If it were, she would produce another kind of misspelling. Instead of ons (once) she might spell it wuns, for example. She's not simply sounding out. She's remembering what words look like and how related words she uses are spelled.

On the next page is a chart showing her conventional and invented spellings:

Invented Spellings				*Conventional Spellings*		
ons (once)	thar (there)		The	8	by
dodre (daughter) 3			old	6	upon
hase (house)	wods (woods)		a/an	5	time
codint (couldn't)			was	2	They
wocke (walk)	wocking (walking)		man	5	that
bracfiste (breakfast)			and	4	had
dinre (dinner)	wen (when)		his	2	give
throe (through)	forist (forest)		lived	2	him
fawnd (found)	lefe (leaf)		in	4	lunch
tock (took)	mans (man's)		so	2	bed
teye (tea) 2	becam (became)		he	2	One
yungre (younger)	yunge (young)		to	2	day
happyule (happily)			she	2	magic
avre (ever)	aftr (after)		it	2	home
yost (used)			put		much
			This		be

Total different words: 25

Total running words: 28

Total different words in text: 57

Total running words in text: 94

Total different words: 32

Total running words: 66

Percent conventionally spelled: 56.14

Percent conventionally spelled: 70.27

It may surprise you that Shoshana has spelled 70% of all the words and 56% of the different words conventionally. Our culture places so much emphasis on conventional spelling that we automatically focus on deviations.

I avoid using the term "correct" for spelling for an important reason. If English spelling had a set of invariant rules that generated all word spellings, then we might be justified in calling a spelling that violated one of those rules "incorrect." But the rules of English spelling are complex and not the same across dialects, and ultimately the conventional spelling for a given word is arbitrary.

All but two of the words Shoshana uses more than once are spelled conventionally — *daughter* and *tea*, both uncommon spelling patterns — and she invents spellings for those. Most of her conventionally spelled words are high-frequency words, not only for her but for the language: articles *the* and *a/an*; pronouns *his, he, she, it, him, they*; prepositions *by, in, to, upon*; other function words *was, and, so, be, that, had, this, much*. She also spells conventionally three less frequent words she uses more than once in the story: *old, man* and *lived*, as well as some she uses only once: *time, give, lunch, bed, home, day, one* and *magic*.

Her only invented spellings for function words are *there, ever, when, through* and *after*.

She tries some invention on words ending with /r/: for *daughter (dodre), dinner, (dinre), younger (yungre)* and *ever (avre)* she uses <re> as the British do in *centre* and *theatre*. She doesn't use the conventional rule here, but she does have a rule, one that is possible and one that provides an excellent example of how readers invent rules. She's likely aware that there's an <e> in words like these, and is simply putting it after the <r> instead of before, as she would after the <l> in words like *little* and *bottle* which use <e> as a final marker. For *thar* and *aftr* she uses a different rule: an <r> by itself looks right.

Her other invented spellings also show that Shoshana has used her own rules to produce spellings that are possible, if not conventional. Some of her rules are easy to identify. For instance, except for *becam*, she consistently adds a final <e> to words like *hase, wocke* (dropping it for *wocking*), *bracfiste, throe, lefe* and *teye*. *Once* she spells *ons*, relating it to her conventional spelling of *one*. In most instances she shows the influence not only of how words sound to her, but also of how they look in print.

This story reveals clearly that Shoshana has invented a spelling system that includes phonics and other strategies she uses in her writing. She already spells most of the frequent words of English conventionally, and her personal rules produce comprehensible and possible English spellings. She uses her memory of how words look as well as how they sound in inventing spellings.

Perhaps the most important thing she shows, however, is that she isn't afraid to use words she needs in her writing even though she still can't spell them conventionally. This one story doesn't provide sufficient evidence by itself, of course, but it's reasonable to infer that she's moving toward conventional spelling, since she already spells 70% of the words she needs for this story conventionally.

On the next page is an earlier letter, written when Shoshana was seven. This is a different genre, but it's obvious that she controls it as well. Written conventionally, it says:

Dear Gramma,

I hope you are feeling better. I hope you will like my letter. Say "I love you" to Grampa for me. I love you, too.

Love,

Shoshana

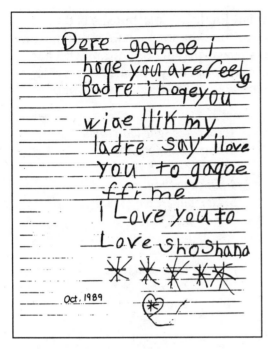

At the bottom she's added marks for love and kisses, a non-alphabetic convention to represent her feelings as she writes.

Notice that she knows the proper letter form: start with *Dear* . . . and end with *Love* . . . She uses some conventional spellings: *I, you, are, my, say, love, me.* She also spells *hope* conventionally, although she's reversed the line on the <p>. She does that in grampa (*gapoe*) too. She shows progress from the letter to the story in every respect, yet her strategies for inventing spellings are clearly visible in her earlier writing.

Here is a sample of another genre produced by this writer shortly after the letter. It was placed on her apartment door to welcome guests as they arrived for a Halloween party. It reads:

Please enter to the party. I will be Tigerlily and Noah will be an Indian.
Shoshana Castro.

A speech balloon surrounds the text and is connected to the mouth of the accompanying self-portrait. In this text, periods, which she didn't include in the letter, end each sentence. Again some function words have conventional spellings and spellings of the other words are plausible. *Will* is spelled conventionally here, but *wiae* in the letter.

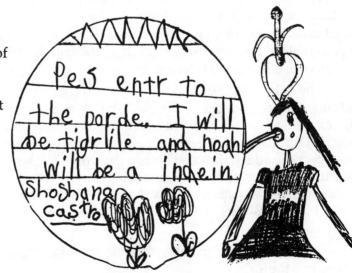

Shoshana grew up in a bilingual Spanish-English home, but she had no instruction in Spanish literacy. When she was nine she spent about six months in the Colombian Andes. One evening when she was playing restaurant with her six-year-old brother she announced she would speak only Spanish. She wrote this menu at that time, her first written Spanish text. The English is my poor translation.

1. Cow's tongue with salad
2. Meat with tomatoes
3. Chicken with rice
4. Duck with salsa (sauce)
5. Hamburger with potatoes
6. Rice with fish

and to drink

1. passion fruit
2. pineapple
3. orange
4. Coca Cola
5. chocolate
6. lemonade

1 Lengwe con de bake enselatha
2. corna con tomates
3 poyoe con arse
4 poto con solsa
5 amdargsa con papase
6 aros con pescato

y pod tomre

1 modakx
2 pena
3 nadanha
4 cokola
5 choklata
6 Lamanatha

She uses some of her English spelling conventions: <w> for the sound she hears in *Lengua* (tongue), for instance. She spells the consonant she hears in *ensalada* (salad) and *limonada* (lemonade) with a <th>, producing *enselatha* and *lamanatha*, because the Spanish /d/ is closer to the sound she hears in *the*. She spells *por* (for) *pod*, and *naranha* (orange) *nadanha*, because the Spanish /r/ is fricative like /d/ and /t/ in English.

She's also aware that, in some Spanish spellings, <ll> and <y> represent the same sound. So she spells *pollo* (chicken) *poyoe*. She tries two spellings for *arros* (rice): *arse* and *aros*. Interestingly, although Spanish doesn't use the silent <e> at the ends of words, she uses it in *poyoe, arse, papase* (potatoes) and *tomre* (to drink). I suspect she added the <e> because the words she wrote looked too short, and she used her English spelling reasoning: maybe there's a silent <e>. Notice, though, that she spells *vaca* (cow) *bake*; /b/ and /v/ have essentially the same sound in Spanish, and at the end of a Spanish word <e> sounds like /ay/ in English.

I've included this menu with Shoshana's invented spellings in Spanish to show two things:

➤ that she is drawing on her English phonics and spelling strategies while at the same time developing specifically Spanish ones;

➤ that invented spellings aren't unique to English.

Invented spellings occur in the writing of developing writers in all languages. All languages have dialect differences. All languages have alternate spellings for the same sound sequences. In writing any alphabetic language, using the phonic relationships will get you to a *comprehensible* spelling — but it won't produce *conventional* spelling. Conventional spelling is arbitrary in all languages.

Summary

The young readers and writers I refer to in this book, and the many others I've studied, have taught me two things about how children develop as readers and writers:

➤ They use both conventional spelling and personal phonics rules for making sense in their reading and writing.

➤ They learn to use phonics *in the process* of reading and writing.

There is no doubt in my mind, based on a rich storehouse of evidence of this kind, that readers and writers learn to control the complex phonic relationships of an alphabetic language like English in the course of learning how to make sense during reading and writing. That's the only way beginners can learn phonics in any useful and productive way. And, not surprisingly, it's the same way they learn oral language, which hearing children have already accomplished long before they learn how to read and write.

6

*Real
children's
books, with their
authentic texts, are what
children check their
invented spellings
against.*

The roots of literacy

Children in modern societies grow up surrounded by functional, meaningful print. If that print is non-alphabetic, as in China and Japan, the children very early learn the meanings of the most common characters in the contexts in which they experience them. They also learn the names of some of these characters, and something about the strokes and components they consist of. They begin to play at writing and are particularly interested in how their names are written. In Japan, most children come to school already on their way to making sense of the complex system used to write Japanese, a non-alphabetic language that consists both of syllabic characters, which mostly represent function words, and of Chinese ideographs, which mostly represent content words.

English-speaking children, too, begin to make sense of the rich functional print around them long before they attend school. They know the meaning of a stop sign, for example, and the logos that signify McDonald's hamburgers, Crest toothpaste and the countless other products that affect their lives. And they know that it's the print that carries the meaning.

At this early stage, their language consists of both a meaning level and an orthographic level. Like Japanese readers, they relate print directly to meaning. But at the same time they learn the names, shapes and formation of letters and become aware that letters come together to form words. They also become interested in how their own names are written and begin to play at writing.

In this example Melissa, a preschooler, writes her name and then uses mostly the letters of her name to represent her message.

Yetta Goodman and many others have focused on the roots of literacy in English. Here is how she summarizes her research:

"The child learns how to mean through written as well as spoken language. Initially, as children interact with the literacy events and implements in their culture, they grow curious and form hypotheses about their functions and purposes. They discover . . . that *written language makes sense*. It communicates or says something. As this generalization begins to develop, children also become concerned with the organization of written language in terms of *how it makes sense*. They begin to find stability and order in the form of written language in the everyday context of its functional use. As these two generalizations are developing, children discover that *they can make sense through written language* as they use it themselves. They develop control or ownership of the strategies of comprehension and composition similar to those they have used in oral language." (Goodman, 1984, pp. 102-103)

Not all children have extensive early experiences with books, even in literate societies, but they all grow up in a print-rich environment. Young children are so much aware of print around them that they almost universally use capital letters — the forms or allographs they most commonly see on signs, billboards, packaging and other environmental print — when they begin to experiment with writing. They may also play with cursive and other forms of writing, however.

Most children try a number of ideas for understanding how specific print relates to meaning and to oral language. When Emilia Ferreiro (1982) studied Spanish- and French-speaking readers, for example, she found that children often go through a phase of thinking that the size of a printed word relates to the size of the object it represents. Their mother's name must be bigger than theirs and their father's even bigger, they reason.

Goodman puts it this way:

"Children learn to relate print to meaning and, where necessary, to oral language. They develop the knowledge that some unit of written language represents some unit of meaning. Although this relationship may include words or letters, it also includes propositions, ideas, concepts, images, signs, symbols, and icons. . . . The developing writer and reader comes to know the relationships between writing, . . . oral language, and the orthography." (pp.105-106)

Children understand very early that it's print readers use to make sense and that print is read horizontally. As they test out their ideas within this understanding, they often start with the concept that each letter represents a whole word or a syllable. If we show some children a box of Kellogg's Corn Flakes, they may tell us the print says "cereal." If we ask them where it says cereal, they're likely to sweep a hand horizontally across the print from left to right, saying "cee-ree-ull" for the three words on the box.

In her study of Chinese preschool print awareness, Lianju Lee (1989) also found children who expected each character to represent a syllable. In Chinese (but not Japanese), that works out quite well. Each character does in fact represent a syllable, and words are represented by one or more characters, depending on how many syllables they contain. On this Peacock Crackers package, the three characters in the bottom left corner say *crackers*. One of Lee's four-year-olds reads them as "cookies." But in Chinese that's a two-syllable word, so she changed her mind: "It says Peacock cookies."

The following examples show one child's movement from syllabic to alphabetic writing.

The first example, which Hannah wrote in February, in kindergarten, uses all capital letters and is basically syllabic.

The second, which she wrote in May is more alphabetic. It includes most consonants and some vowels.

In both cases what Hannah said she wrote was: "Ice cream is good."

In English, writing usually starts with consonants; in Spanish, with vowels. Word and syllabic inventions are the beginning of phonics, even though the children don't yet understand the alphabetic principle: that letter patterns relate to sound patterns (not individual letters to individual sounds). Eventually, as they continue to try to make sense of written language, young readers and writers discover this principle and begin to do two things:

➤ They remember what written words look like.

➤ They develop their own rules for how the spellings relate to how the words sound.

As in all language learning, they overgeneralize the rules at first, producing the types of invented spellings we saw earlier in Shoshana's writing.

Because young children have keen hearing and perceptions that are freer than ours (we know more about what we *should* be seeing and hearing), they often represent sounds too well in their invented spelling. In a book he wrote at home entitled "How to Make Applesauce," Joshua, a beginning first grader, spelled *make* as *mach*. As he finished writing the word he said, "I know there's a 'h.' It's a small sound at the end you can hardly hear." Phonologists tell us that this form of /k/ is aspirated before a vowel. Joshua, whose last name is Hood, already knows that patterns with aspiration can be spelled with <h>.

Since children create these rules for themselves, they freely revise them or set them aside if they don't work. They use their memory of how words look as a check on their inventions — which is why it's important that they both read *and* write as they learn written language. Because they check their invented spellings against the spellings they find in their reading, the authentic texts found in real children's books are the real basis of their growing awareness of spelling conventions. They invent rules that link sound systems and writing systems and test those out in their reading and writing too. And in the process of balancing personal invention and social convention they develop their personal phonics as they attempt to make sense of and through written language.

I said earlier that beginning readers and writers start out with two levels of language: meaning and orthography. To move ahead, they must develop the middle, lexico-grammatical level: the system of language that relates the parts to the meaningful whole. It is no accident that children learn how the spelling system works — how the orthography relates to the phonology — at the same time as they are learning how whole ideas and narratives, not just things, are represented in print. As they try to make sense in their writing, they need to spell the necessary words. As they try to make sense in their reading, they see how words and letters are patterned in texts. In the same way that they learned to make sense in oral language, they learn to make sense of print. And in the process, they learn phonics.

The separate roots of literacy must merge for children to be able to use just enough phonic information — not too little and not too much. And in order to develop proper phonics, beginning literates must develop generalizations about how the orthography of English works in real texts, not in the artificial language of many classroom programs. That knowledge is necessary for but not the same as their knowledge of phonics: how orthography relates to phonology.

Consider, for instance, the convention that English words don't end in <v>; the final <e> in *have, live, salve,* etc. is there only to satisfy that convention. And, inevitably, conventions sometimes clash. *Dove/dove* are homographs: in one, the <e> follows the vowel/consonant/<e> pattern, and in the other, the <e> is a marker to avoid ending the word with <v>. The only way we can dependably differentiate *dove/dove* is in texts where the whole makes clear the nature of the parts: *The dove dove through the window.*

In learning to speak and understand speech, we learn to control the sound system, the phonology of our language(s). In learning to read and write, we learn to control the orthography. And in becoming literate in an alphabetic language, we learn to control the phonics, the relationships between orthography and phonology. As we learn, we produce some unconventional language and try some unconventional "rules." But only by learning to read and write *while we read and write authentic written language* do we become fully effective and move toward social conventions.

Invented and conventional spelling

Invention is both natural and necessary in all language learning.

The grapho-phonic, lexico-grammatical and semantic-pragmatic cue systems must all become integrated in reading and writing, as they already are in oral language, for readers to make sense of unfamiliar print and for writers to express meaning comprehensibly. The best evidence of the development of phonics generalizations in young literates resides in their invented spellings as they seek to say something through writing.

I hope by now I've established that invention is both natural and necessary in language learning. And I hope I've convinced you that developing writers must invent spellings for words they need as they write. Young writers simply can't learn to write freely and productively if they're always confined to words they know they can spell conventionally.

But do children ever become conventional spellers if they are permitted to continue to invent spellings as they write? The results of a two-year study of the writing development of Tohono O'Odham (native American) third and fourth grade learners (Goodman and Wilde, 1992) showed that these children spelled a significantly larger percentage of an increasing number of words conventionally by the end of the study. They used more different words and wrote more in fourth grade than in third, and yet the percentage of conventionally spelled words increased in the second year.

Percentage of Conventional Spelling: Years I and II		N=13,793 Words
	Year I	Year II
Elaine	80.8	78.0
Anna	82.6	85.4
Gordon	79.4	89.1
Rachel	85.2	86.2
Vincent	81.8	87.0
Dana	94.5	95.4
6 children	84.6	87.6

The table above shows what appears to be a modest increase from 84.6% to 87.6%, but considering that they wrote almost 14 000 words, that difference is statistically significant. It's not likely it could be an accidental finding.

These six children showed better than 85% conventional spelling over the two years. Furthermore, with the exception of Elaine, they were significantly more conventional in fourth grade. While Elaine appears to have declined somewhat, the quality of her non-conventional spelling improved. In her non-conventional words she spelled more parts conventionally.

Notice also that Gordon, who had the lowest percentage of conventional spelling in the first year, improved from 79.4% to 89.1% conventional in the second year.

The study also showed that words used more frequently were more likely to be spelled conventionally: words used 100 or more times were 97.5% conventional, while words used only once were only 44.8% conventional. Goodman explains:

> "It makes sense that children are more likely to know how to spell words that they use more frequently and that they won't know how to spell words that they haven't used before. If children are continuing to grow as writers, to explore new topics using new vocabulary, they will continue to have a certain percent of invented spellings. A child who always spells perfectly is not taking very many risks." (Goodman et al., 1984a, p. IV-11)

All of the young writers in the study became more conventional in their non-conventional spelling, evident in how they spelled selected features across words. Wilde, using the same data, reports that over the two years the children spelled short vowels (as in *cat, bed, hit, pop, cut*), 94.4% conventionally. Not surprisingly, unstressed vowels that take the schwa sound were less conventionally spelled, though even those were 74% conventional in the third grade, 83% in the fourth. Since phonics is of no help in predicting how any particular unstressed oral vowel will appear in spelling, it must be that the increasing tendency toward conventional spelling results from other inputs — from more extensive reading and memory of how words look, for instance.

Wilde also studied the spelling of the <ed> past tense suffix, which went from 51% conventional in third grade to 71% in fourth. Here's a case where following a simple phonic rule produces unconventional spelling. The spelling system tends to keep the <ed> spelling even when the sound shifts, depending on how the base ends, as in *walked, joined, painted*. The unconventional spellings were usually phonic: *wacht* (watched), *calld* (called).

Many other studies show the same move towards conventionality in spelling, as measured by the increasing numbers of words, percentage of words and number of orthographic features that are represented conventionally. In spelling as in all language, development results from both invention and convention and should be seen as approaching equilibrium between the two.

So, while phonics does play a role in spelling, it's a limited role. It's not only unreliable in itself, it's also constrained by other influences involved in producing conventional spellings.

Dialect in spelling

Read (1986) summarizes studies that support the expectation that varied pronunciations in different dialects are reflected in spelling, particularly in younger children. He says, however:

"... it is a mistake to assume that the phonetic strategies operate alone at any level of spelling development. While phonetic input is primary in the early years, a child later acquires a repertoire of strategies based on morphology and graphemic conventions; these strategies then play a greater role in spelling." (p. 74)

Dialect is reflected in reading as well. Our miscue studies with several dialect groups showed that they could all deal with the dialects of the stories they read. Dialect became a "problem" only if the teacher rejected the dialect-based pronunciations of the readers, confusing them about whether their reading was successful.

Read confirms that, even though there is dialect influence on invented spelling, the movement toward conventional spelling is much the same across all dialect groups. Again, problems arise only if developing writers are confused by the rejection of their dialect-based inventions and the imposition of phonic rules that don't fit the phonology of their dialects.

Deaf readers and writers

Deaf learners learn to read and write an oral language as a second language.

Some people are born profoundly deaf, and their language learning is necessarily different from that of hearing people — and also from that of deaf people who lost their hearing after developing oral language. Those who can hear learn an oral language easily and naturally. Those who can't hear can't learn oral language in hearing families.

But that doesn't mean they can't learn language. In fact, if they are fortunate enough to be among signing people, they learn it just as easily as hearing children do. Deaf children who are not in signing homes do invent language, like all children, but they don't have access to the social speech conventions that would shape their inventions toward the spoken language. They experience a good deal of frustration as they try to understand and be understood by others.

The sign languages of deaf people aren't simply representations of oral languages; they are completely different languages. Visible signs, usually made with hands and arms in the cube of three dimensional space between "speaker" and "listener," are the symbols of sign languages. Usually those signs are ideographic: each sign represents an idea. One sign may represent shooting an arrow, another shooting a gun. Grammar is also different in American sign language than it is in English. The sign for past tense, for example, applies to all the following verbs unless another sign says it doesn't.

For the deaf, alphabetic writing systems don't relate to the phonology of the oral language in any useful way. Deaf learners learn to read and write an oral language as a second language, not as a second form of a first language, as hearing learners do. They must learn the language, including its grammar and vocabulary, *while* they learn to read and write.

In one respect they actually have an advantage in learning to read and write: if they know a sign language, they already control one visual language. Furthermore, users of American Sign Language (ASL) use finger spellings, signs for the letters of a written word, to sign words for which they have no specific sign. Where the finger spelling is an easy sequence, they may use letter signs even when there is a sign for the word. That means that deaf children learning to read and write are likely to know and use a number of finger-spelled words in their everyday sign communication.

There is no reason why deaf pupils can't learn to read and write English. But we must understand that English is a second language for them and one quite different from their likely first language. We must also understand that alphabetic writing offers different features for deaf users than for hearing ones:

➤ their first language is ideographic;

➤ their finger spellings simply provide a supplementary system;

➤ they can't hear the sounds of oral language.

So there's no point in teaching any kind of phonics to them. (I'm stating the obvious here because, believe it or not, deaf kids have suffered through phonics programs!) Rather, to help deaf learners become literate in English, we must relate sign and written English through the meanings they represent.

Summary

Perhaps we can draw this final conclusion, based on what we know about how deaf readers and writers learn and use English: *it is possible to read and write English without phonics.* Deaf people do it all the time. Written language represents meaning, and meaning is what makes it possible for readers to make sense of written language. Hearing people may use oral language to support their making sense of print, but they possess all the same tools as the deaf do for successful reading and writing without the oral component, and therefore without phonics.

With this last paragraph I have come to the end of my first task in this book, to present the "science" of phonics. I've demonstrated my understanding of phonics as the third graphophonic system: the link between phonology (the system of sounds) and orthography (the system of written symbols). I've acknowledged that language is complex, that sound and print information is often ambiguous, but that even the youngest of young children are marvelous language learners. I've shown that the real roots of literacy are to be found in genuine literacy experiences.

At the beginning of this book I promised that I would also consider the case of those who advocate that young children receive direct instruction about phonics — that is, explicit instruction in phonics rules. I'll do that in the following two chapters. First, I'll consider their claims in detail and explain why I can't accept them. Then, given the frequent media attention phonics attracts, and the tireless efforts of "phonics-first" pressure groups in the United States, Canada and other areas of the English-speaking world, I feel it's important to comment, as well, on the politics of phonics.

7

*My view
of how phonics
is learned rests on
my personal belief that
children's learning is
a social-personal
invention.*

Learning about phonics

Many people say that teaching about phonics is an essential instructional strategy. Among those many are parents concerned about what they see as the failure of schooling for their children, organized lobby and pressure groups in the United States and elsewhere, and newspaper columnists, like Canada's Andrew Nikiforuk, who have made phonics-first their cause. I'll talk about them in greater detail in the next chapter.

In this chapter I want to consider the claims of more sophisticated advocates, especially academics and authors Richard Anderson and Marilyn Adams, who see teaching about phonics as essential for the learning of reading and, to a lesser extent, of writing. Both have made their views known in widely distributed publications.

Before I tackle the specifics of their views of phonics and phonics teaching, however, it's necessary to set the stage by describing some of the many alternate views of human learning, especially language learning, that are advanced today. It isn't necessary, or even possible, to explore them in detail in this book, but we do need to recognize that at least one theory is always present, implicitly or explicitly, in what people say about education and schooling.

I also need to make clear the view of learning that I've come to accept and that underlies my view of how literacy is learned, and how phonics is learned as people become literate.

Views of learning

At least five views of learning regularly show up in the literature on literacy development:

➤ The *innatist view* holds that language isn't learned at all, that in fact humans are born pre-programmed for language, much the way birds and fish are pre-programmed to migrate (nature).

➤ The *behaviorist view* holds that all human learning, including language and literacy learning, is the result of human response to environmental stimuli (nurture).

➤ Piaget's *psychogenetic view* (1971) holds that learning is the active means by which organisms accommodate or assimilate to their environment.

➤ Vygotsky's *social view* (1978) holds that learning is the internalization of social patterns and structures.

➤ Halliday's *functional-systemic view* holds that the form of language evolves from its social function, and is thus a social invention.

My own view combines aspects of Piaget's, Vygotsky's and Halliday's.

Innatist and behaviorist views

I've grouped the innatist and behaviorist views of learning, which otherwise are quite different, because they have in common a passive view of learners. Learners are people to whom things happen (say the innatists) or to whom things are done (say the behaviorists).

In the innatist view, every human brain is pre-programmed with a universal grammar which is expressed in the particular language the child hears as he or she grows up. Most innatists, however, limit what is universally innate to oral language which, in their view, isn't learned at all. For most of these people, written language isn't really language but a secondary representation of it. Many linguists, particularly Noam Chomsky (1965) and his associates and followers, are innatists, and most of them have shown little interest in written language *per se*. Steven Krashen (1985), a linguist concerned with second language learning, is a notable exception. He postulates a language acquisition device (LAD) that also encompasses written language and argues that written language, like oral, is acquired through comprehensible input. He calls his view a natural approach.

Behaviorists believe that language, like everything else, is learned through a series of direct stimulus-response episodes. The limitations of that simplistic view were recognized when it came to explaining more complex learning, such as language, and many behaviorists have become *connectionists* as a result, in particular, of two relatively recent developments:

➤ Brain research shows that the brain doesn't store memories in single locations, but as *patterns of cell activations.*

➤ Computer simulations of learning have produced "artificial intelligence."

But connectionists still believe that language is learned as a series of recognition processes. And since behavior is thought to be a response to environmental stimuli, teaching remains an *intervention* in the form of stimuli designed to change behavior. In behavioral terms, school learning is activated by direct, explicit instruction with specific behavioral objectives and assessed by criterion-referenced instruments.

Most advocates of phonics programs hold behavioristic views of learning, views that justify a hierarchical part-to-whole, one-piece-at-a-time approach. In this view, reading and writing must begin with direct instruction of letters and letter-sound relationships and progress to mastering vocabulary a word at a time; only after skills are established can meaningful reading material be introduced. Jeanne Chall (1983) lays out explicit stages of development (really stages of instruction) that follow this skill hierarchy movement from code to meaning.

I often find confusion in behavioral reading programs between instruction and learning. If children perform the acts instruction requires of them, can we necessarily assume they have learned? Many advocates of phonics "programs" like those endorsed by the phonics-first lobby are convinced that learning theory is simply something eggheads fight about. From their point of view kids learn only what they're explicitly taught. So the question of teaching vs. learning isn't worth fussing about.

Marilyn Adams is an experimental psychologist who has risen to recent prominence with her book *Beginning to Read* (1990), which mixes behaviorist and innatist views. She accepts the innatist view of oral language acquisition:

> ". . . In speaking and listening, our attention is focused on the task of comprehending — of making sense out of the collective, ordered stream of words. To focus instead on each individual word, syllable, or phoneme would be counter-productive. Even ignoring issues of comprehension, it would be too time-consuming; we would quickly lose track of the rest of the spoken stream. For purposes of listening to language, therefore, it is fortunate that the processing of subunits — phonemes, syllables, and words — is automatic." (p. 294)

In Adams' view, it's possible to focus on comprehending rather than sub-units in listening only because oral language doesn't have to be learned. In a footnote on the same page, she informs her readers that speech scientists have proven that:

"... if phonemes arrived as discrete acoustical segments, the speed ...
would exceed the temporal resolving power of the human ear. Speech
would sound like an unanalyzable buzz."

That sounds very much like the description I've given of how readers make
sense of *print*, but Adams immediately adds:

"For purposes of learning to read or write, however, these subunits must be
dug out of their normal, subattentional status. Children must push their
attention down from the level of comprehension at which it normally
works." (pp. 294-295)

She's saying that making sense of speech holistically is natural. But for kids
to learn to read, they must be taught to do something which is unnatural: focus
on words, syllables and phonemes rather than meaning, because written
language isn't innate, like oral language.

I'll come back to this issue later, but I need to point out a major
inconsistency in her arguments. If the speed of speech is too fast for listeners to
resolve discrete acoustic segments, how then can the ability to comprehend
written language (or even recognize words) be dependent on attending to
phonemes? Silent reading, even for non-speed readers, is far faster than the
speed of speech!

Holistic views

I've grouped three views of learning here — Piaget's, Vygotsky's and
Halliday's — because they too, whatever their differences, have something in
common: they all believe that learners actively seek to make sense of the world.
People expect the world to make sense; they keep constructing their view of it
and then assimilating or accommodating their constructions as they try them out.

Piagetian Emilia Ferreiro and a group of international colleagues have
studied young children's literacy development in several languages and
orthographies. They provide a view of children as learners making sense of the
print in their environment well before and independent of any instruction.
Ferreiro rejects the notion of children needing to be taught phonics, word parts
or word recognition. She sees children making sense of print just as they earlier
made sense of oral language, by meeting it whole, and she questions the value of
phonics/deciphering:

"The routine nature of this practice responds to methodological principles
derived from empiricist conceptions of learning. School is directed toward
passive children who know nothing, who must be taught. It is not directed
toward active children who not only pose their own problems but
spontaneously construct mechanisms for solving them, who reconstruct the

object [written language] to appropriate it through the development of knowledge and not through the exercise of skills." (Ferreiro and Teberosky, 1982, p. 281)

Ferreiro quotes the French educator Foucambert:

". . . reading consists of selecting information from written language to construct meaning directly." (p. 275)

Vygotsky's learning theory is a more social one. In his view, the language that surrounds the child is internalized and becomes the language of thought and learning as well as communication:

"The teaching of writing has been conceived in narrowly practical terms. Children are taught to trace out letters and make words out of them, but they are not taught written language. The mechanics of reading what is written are so emphasized that they overshadow written language as such." (1978, p. 105)

The linguist Halliday also has a social view of learning. He chose *Learning How to Mean* as the title of the book that describes his study of his own son's language development because he believes that, as we learn language, we learn how our society uses language to organize meaning and symbolically represent the world and our experiences with it — learning, therefore, is a social-personal invention. The form of language evolves from its social function, and the universals of language stem from the universality of social functions, not from any innate grammar or LAD.

Halliday sees oral and written language as parallel and applies his analysis to both. Each serves a set of functions and overlapping sets of genres; some genres are exclusively oral, some written and some both:

"We all use language for many different purposes, in a wide variety of contexts. And some of these purposes are such that they cannot be adequately served by language in its spoken form; we need writing. The impetus for reading and writing is a functional one, just as the impetus for learning to speak and listen was in the first place. We learn to speak because we want to do things that we cannot do otherwise; and we learn to read and write for the same reason." (1972, p. iv)

My own view

My own view of learning builds on Piaget, Vygotsky and Halliday. I see children constructing their understandings of the world and their responses to it in the context of the culture they belong to. And I see them as actively inventing language as they need it, but doing so in the context of the language of their home and community. Children who grow up in a literate environment (most children in the modern world) have begun to become literate long before they come to school. The dynamic dialectic between personal invention and social convention is the dominant force in language and literacy development, as it is in all learning.

I strongly believe that the invention-convention theory of language covers both written and oral language development, as my own research on the reading process demonstrates. What Adams sees as happening in listening is precisely what I found happening in reading as well. Readers keep their attention on comprehension, just as listeners do, and shift their focus to the details of the text and the cue systems they are using only when comprehension begins to break down. They come to control the parts and the relationships among them as they learn to make sense of the whole.

I want to link the examples from the earlier discussion of my miscue studies to an important aspect of language learning that often gets overlooked: *the most important language phenomena are not directly observable in the language that we hear.* We don't hear phonemes. We hear sounds, and we must organize those sounds into patterned language to make sense of them. We must invent for ourselves the significant units — phonemes — and learn what features of the sounds are significant and non-significant for each phoneme. Furthermore, we must do all this from the otherwise formless flow of sound that reaches our ears, even though particular sounds may be changed by what follows and precedes them, and allophones may exist in different positions in the stream, and the significant features of sounds may change as we assign the phonemes.

The grammar of the language and its rules are not observable either. We must invent those too, and then apply our inventions back to what we hear to check out their validity. We must even infer where words begin and end. In connected speech we don't have time gaps equivalent to the spaces that print uses to mark off words in connected speech. And the same process of invention is at work in learning to read and write — the same remarkable human ability to invent and test our inventions against the social conventions — as was demonstrated by the young readers and writers in my studies.

For Adams, nothing can be learned from the study of oral language development that is useful for understanding literacy development. Learning to speak just happens; learning to read and write is an achievement. But in fact, learning oral language is the greater accomplishment, because it starts with nothing. Children learning to read and write have their well-developed oral language learning to draw on. Written language is less, not more abstract than oral language from the learners' perspective, because they already control the syntactic and semantic systems of the language they are learning to read and write.

From a holistic view, on the other hand, learning to read and write is a matter of learning to comprehend written language. It involves learning to apply the psycholinguistic strategies already learned in listening, with orthographic rather than phonological input. Children learn first from contextualized environmental print, and then from books and other less contextualized print. Their learning, in and out of school, blossoms when they meet complete texts that are interesting, meaningful and relevant for them.

It's not only unnecessary and unnatural to teach children to read letter by letter, but it's unproductive as well.

We learn to read and write, as we learn to speak and listen, from whole to part, not from part to whole. Only when we can comprehend the whole are we fully able to see how the parts relate to it. Kids who can read are usually good at learning phonics, because they can put phonic relationships into the context of making sense of print.

Research on literacy learning

In the preceding section I contrasted my views of language learning with those of one of the current powerful advocates of teaching about phonics. I presented my evidence earlier, especially in the samples of children's miscues and invented spellings. So then, what evidence does Adams cite to prove that phonemic awareness and phonics instruction are necessary to learning to read?

She lays the foundation for her views about systematic phonics teaching in what she says about her learning theory:

"Among theories and models, the connectionist framework meets and explains the data on human word recognition performance exceptionally well. It is for this reason alone that I have adopted it in this book." (p. 201)

These premises underlie Adams' very thorough summation of the research literature:

➤ Oral language is innate but written language is learned, as connectionists have described learning.

➤ So written language, unlike oral language, must be taught.

➤ Reading is word recognition.

➤ Skillful reading (word recognition) involves "relatively complete processing of individual letters." (p. 105)

➤ Research shows young children are not "phonemically aware" and can't easily recognize individual letters and match phonemes with letters.

➤ Direct instruction in phonics and letter-by-letter reading is necessary.

Based on those premises, she thoroughly summarizes all the research on processing individual letters to recognize words. But she doesn't deal with the research on how children learn to make sense of natural texts, how they develop the ability to do in reading what she acknowledges they can do in listening: attend to the task of comprehending. And she makes an unwarranted logical leap when she assumes that children can and must be taught to do what she acknowledges it is difficult for them to learn: phonics, which to her is matching phonemes and letters.

The problem is that all she's done is summarize studies of how words are recognized and how children can best be taught to recognize them — not how readers and writers make sense of written language and how kids learn to do that.

Her studies show kids learning phonics as a prerequisite for learning to recognize words. In her view phonics and phonemic awareness are necessary but hard-to-learn abstractions. She agrees that "children have a highly developed knowledge of phonemes long before they learn to read" (p. 305), yet she believes this functional knowledge is insufficient. Children must be taught what they haven't learned: how to abstract the specific phonemes out of language and relate them to the letters, each individually recognized.

My research shows that kids learn to use phonological, orthographic and phonic information, along with syntactic and semantic information, as they try to make sense of print. In the same way as they learned how to use phonology to make sense of speech, they come to control functional (not decontextualized and over-valued) phonic knowledge in the context of learning to read and write. There is no need to require kids to do unnatural abstract analysis as a prerequisite to recognizing words as a prerequisite to comprehending!

(A key factor in how we view phonics is our understanding of how children learn oral language. I can't summarize all the research on language development here, but you'll find a very complete explanation in Halliday's *Learning How to Mean*.)

A house divided

You have before you two very distinct positions, and many of you may feel a sense of bewilderment about how to choose between them. In this section I want to take a much closer look at the claims of those who advocate instruction about phonics, because it's my claim that they have skirted the real issues of language learning, a claim I want to demonstrate by looking closely at their own writings.

Adams is not the only prominent academic with this view of phonics. Richard Anderson is a well-known psychologist who heads the Center for the

Study of Reading at the University of Illinois. In 1985 the Center produced a report called *Becoming a Nation of Readers* that gives "clear support of 'phonics first and fast'," according to David Pearson in his foreword to Adams' *Beginning to Read*. (p. 1)

Although the report professes a view of reading as meaning construction, it unequivocally states that "every reader must break the code that relates spelling to sound and meaning." (p. 12) It also states that readers must be able to "decode words quickly and accurately." (p. 11) Phonics is defined as "instruction in the relationship between letters and speech sounds" (p. 38), and that instruction should be given early, be explicit and be kept simple. (pp. 43, 57)

Interestingly, although both Anderson and Adams have given great aid and comfort to the political advocates of phonics-first reading instruction (see pp. 98-104), both of their reports actually voice strong reservations about the value of direct instruction in letter-sound relationships in reading instruction.

Here is what the Anderson report says:

". . . a number of reading programs, including ones not known for providing intensive phonics, try to teach too many letter-sound relationships and phonics instruction drags out over too many years. These programs seem to be making the dubious assumption that exposure to a vast set of phonics relationships will enable a child to produce perfect pronunciations of words. The more reasonable assumption is that phonics can help the child come up with approximate pronunciations — candidates that have to be checked to see whether they match words known from spoken language that fit in the context of the story being read." (p. 35)

". . . Once the basic relationships have been taught, the best way to get the children to knowledge of letter-sound correspondences is through repeated opportunities to read." (p. 38)

And here are Adams' conclusions:

"Ideas that appear to be elegantly simple and powerful from the vantage point of the armchair often lose their gleam under the close lens of implementation. Letter-sound instruction seems to be a case in point.

"First, correspondences between letters and sounds are not one to one. Instead they are one to several in both directions, spoiling the tidiness or simplicity of the 'hierarchy.' Second, this diminution in the simplicity of the system brings with it a diminution in its power. Where once the goal was (glibly) cast as one of teaching the children the correct sound for each letter, it turns out to be one of teaching them a whole set of possible sounds for each letter." (p. 255)

Are Adams and Anderson insincere, then, in their advocacy of early phonics instruction? Not exactly. Both statements are consistent with what is central in their respective views of the reading process. Within their own views (and they don't always agree with each other), these authors conclude that phonics, even as they define it, is not a simple, easily taught set of correspondences.

Anderson defines reading from his perspective as a researcher of comprehension:

> "Reading is the process of constructing meaning from written texts. It is a complex skill requiring the coordination of a number of interrelated sources of information . . . reading is a holistic act. In other words, while reading can be analyzed into subskills such as discriminating letters and identifying words, performing the subskills one at a time does not constitute reading. Reading can be said to take place only when the parts are put together in a smooth, integrated performance." (p. 7)

That may sound quite compatible with my view of reading, but it isn't, because it still sees the whole as the sum of discrete parts, even though those parts must operate together for comprehension to occur. That's not a small difference either, because it leads to very different views of how the whole is brought together.

In Anderson's view, quick and accurate word identification is necessary to comprehension — quick and accurate enough to facilitate making sense of the text. That's enough justification for arguing that starting with phonics is esssential to reading, but it also implies that phonics is not sufficient for either recognizing words or making sense of printed texts. Anderson explicitly rejects the view that reading proceeds letter by letter or word by word:

> "It has been known since late in the 19th century that short, familiar words can be read as fast as single letters and that, under some conditions, words can be identified when the separate letters cannot be. These facts would be impossible if the first step in word identification were always identification of the constituent letters and their sounds." (p. 11)

Adams departs from Anderson on this point. She believes that the whole is the sum of its parts and that every word is recognized and every letter used in successful word recognition:

> "The reading process is driven by the visual recognition of individual letters in familiar ordered sequence and is critically supported by the translation of those strings of letters into their phonological correspondences." (p. 237)

For Adams, reading is reading words. Here is her restatement of the assignment the federal government gave her:

"Before you pick this book up, you should understand fully that the topic
at issue is that of reading words. Before you put this book down, however,
you should understand fully that the ability to read words, quickly,
accurately, and effortlessly, is critical to skillful reading comprehension —
in the obvious ways and in a number of more subtle ones." (p. 3)

Yet Adams devotes a whole chapter of her book to answering the question
"Why phonics?" Here is her conclusion:

". . . [an] assumption about phonics programs is that, whatever their
method, their success is owed to the importance of teaching children how
to sound words out. . . . it is possible that the ability to sound words out —
even while being an invaluable step toward reading independence — is not
the primary positive outcome of phonic instruction. . . . Laboratory research
indicates that the most critical factor beneath fluent word reading is the
ability to recognize letters, spelling patterns, and whole words effortlessly,
automatically, and visually." (p. 54)

Rather than justifying phonics, Adams' "look-recognize" view justifies a
word-recognition model of reading: the ability to look at words and word parts
and automatically recognize them is the key to reading. At best, phonics is of
limited use in recognizing words.

Let me point out one important difference in how I've been discussing
phonics and how Adams and Anderson view it:

➤ The Anderson-Adams view defines phonics as *instruction about letter-sound
relationships.*

➤ My view defines phonics, for alphabetically written language only, as *the
patterns of relationships between the patterns of speech and the patterns of writing.*

Their definition introduces two problems. In the first place, they imply that
there is a simple set of one-to-one correspondences between letters and sounds.
Although both Adams and Anderson agree that there is no such correspondence,
they continue, in their respective books, to advocate teaching phonics as if there
were, with examples that tend to stay with the simple, "most regular"
relationships that come closest to being one to one.

In the second place, they confuse teaching with what is being taught. They
don't separate letter-sound relationships from programs for teaching them to
children. Virtually all the "phonics research" they summarize took place in either
laboratories or classrooms where research subjects responded to be *being taught*
letter-sound relationships. The confusion is further compounded by assuming
that learning and teaching are reciprocal, and that experiments designed to teach
phonics (defined as letter-sound relationships) can be used to judge how pupils
learn phonics. (My own miscue research, in contrast, has focused not on teaching

but on what children have demonstrated they do while reading, a very different research procedure.)

So both Adams and Anderson dance around their own awareness that letter-sound relationships are not simple, and that attempts to teach them as if they were are not all that successful. Since they accept the "research" that "phonics" (instruction) works, they're left with a dilemma: they must rationalize why a misconception could lead to successful learning. And that gets me into the question of research paradigms.

Contrasting research paradigms

It's more than our views of learning and our conclusions about the relationships of phonics to reading, reading instruction and reading development in language learning that divides the work of Anderson and Adams from my own. We are also divided by our different research paradigms.

Adams has rightly been credited with being marvelously thorough in her distillation and synthesis of the research literature on phonics as it relates to beginning reading. She cites dozens of studies for every aspect she discusses, and hundreds of studies overall. Yet a search of her index reveals that some of the key aspects of English language phonics I have discussed are not present. There are no references in the index to *dialect, stress, perception, intonation, allographs* or *fonts,* for instance.

Indexes don't always fully represent a book, but they always list what the author considers important. The terms I looked for and didn't find are clearly important to me. They clearly aren't important to Adams. There are no references to schwa in the index either, but I looked for and did find one in the text, in this rather strange statement:

> "Lazy mouth (or, more kindly, anticipatory mouth) can generally explain the distributions of *schwa* and of voiced and unvoiced *th* and *s* as well. . . . And it has been demonstrated that even where the unstressed vowels of *polysyllabic* words are normally sounded as *schwa,* children who are taught to pronounce them instead as they are printed learn more about the words' spellings." (pp. 269-270 — the emphasis on *polysyllabic* is mine; it isn't in the index either)

I'm sure that historians will find it interesting to learn that English tongues got lazy during the 14th century when unaccented vowels shifted to schwa. Her terminology is reminiscent of the outrageous explanation that the dialects of African-Americans result from lazy, thick lips and tongues. This also ranks with the quaint notion that Castilian Spanish differs in certain phonemes from other Spanish dialects because a Spanish king had a lisp. It's obvious that Adams didn't research the schwa phenomenon. She doesn't treat it as a significant aspect of English phonics: all vowels reduce to schwa in unaccented syllables, but as a defect of enunciation. No need, then, to explain how it affects reading. (And it's a strange view of instruction that finds value in teaching children to mispronounce words!)

Her index does contain many references to both *letter recognition skills* and *word recognition*, and I wondered how she could deal so extensively with *recognition* and not deal with *perception*. I was able to find uses of both *perceptions* and *perceive* in a discussion of connectionism, the neo-behaviorist learning theory she subscribes to.

"According to connectionist theory, yes, learning accrues through experience. And, yes, our *perceptions* are received by those simple sensory transducers and detectors that we are all innately given." (p. 202)

Here she uses "perceptions" to mean visual inputs. But later in the same discussion she says:

". . . experiences are remembered not in a separate compartment of our heads, but as associated patterns within the very structure of our recognition apparatus. As a result, the way in which we *perceive* the world becomes organized this way as well. We learn to *perceive* the world not as flecks of light and bits of sound, but as parts of patterns that, on their partial activation, recall their balance so as to create expectations, to fill in sensorial blanks, and to guide our responses." (my emphasis.)

At first glance, that certainly sounds like my view of perception as a process of mental construction. But if you examine her language closely, you'll see that her "perception" is part of a recognition apparatus. It's the recognition of letters and words — entities that are somehow fixed — that's important. She doesn't differentiate between what we see and what we perceive, a point I made earlier.

If the purpose of reading is to recognize letters in order to recognize words, then perception isn't a very significant part of recognition. But if the purpose of reading is to make sense, then how we perceive the world leads us to expectations that go beyond letters and words to sentence patterns and text structures, and always toward meaning.

George Miller (1956), a perceptual psycholinguist, demonstrates that what the brain can perceive from what the eye sees depends on what the brain brings to the seeing. In a string of *random letters*, Miller found, we can perceive five letters at a glance, plus or minus two. In a series of *familiar words*, we can perceive the same number of words: five plus or minus two. And in a connected, meaningful written text, we both perceive and understand a sentence or more at a glance.

For years I've been doing the following demonstration. With an overhead projector I briefly expose lines of print, one at a time, ranging from not quite geometric shapes to a complete meaningful English sentence. It demonstrates conclusively that meaningful sentences are easier to perceive than strings of words, which are easier to perceive than words, which are easier to perceive than nonsense words, which are easier to perceive than strings of letters and numerals. Ironically, it's not the line of vaguely geometric figures that's hardest for most people in my audiences, however, but the line of Hebrew, which is of course quite easily perceived by anyone literate in Hebrew, even without the vowels. The features of Hebrew letters are quite abstract, although no more abstract than Roman letters.

The missing index items demonstrate that Adams is highly selective in what she considers important. She decides importance in terms of her view of reading as sequential recognition of letters and words. But her decisions are also shaped by her view of research, her research paradigm.

Adams deals extensively with two kinds of research:

➤ The first focuses on the use of instructional programs, particularly those that teach phonics directly.

➤ The second is the "rigorous" laboratory research that carefully controls all variables so that each important component of word recognition can be examined.

In her studies of instructional programs, the experimental group gets an experimental program, and the control group gets one labeled "traditional," "regular" or "conventional." Pre-tests and post-tests are administered, and if the experimental group is more successful, statistically speaking, it's assumed that the program has produced the success. Adams reports these studies in great detail, finds them problematic in many respects as individual efforts but accepts their aggregate conclusion that phonics, whatever it is, works. She carefully steps around her own view, which is that it's not so much phonics *per se* as attention to the detail of letters and words that's really being learned in phonics programs.

It's the second type of research Adams apparently feels more comfortable with, however. The key to this kind of research is reducing what is studied so there can be no confusion about the result. That's why most of the studies focus on monosyllabic words; polysyllabic words would complicate them. It's also why subjects are often tested on their ability to apply their "learning" to one-syllable nonsense words, to avoid the possibility that they may already know the "target" words.

Researchers who confine their studies to single-syllable words out of context, or at best in highly reduced contexts, don't have to worry about vowels that reduce to schwa. Monosyllabic words in lists get the same word stress, so there's no worry about vowels changing as stress shifts. There's no worry either about morphophonemic shifts.

While she recognizes the complexities of letter-sound correspondences, Adams and the researchers she summarizes simply ignore the issue of font differences in their research. They draw conclusions about letter recognition, but which allograph (alternate form of the letter) is being recognized? Obviously, the one the stimulus materials in the study are printed in. But then how do kids learn to deal with all the other possible fonts and treat them as perceptually interchangeable?

The absence of any reference to dialect difference in the research she summarizes is even more problematic. Did these researchers choose to use only middle-class subjects who spoke the locally standard dialect? Or did they ignore differences in dialect among their subjects to avoid complicating the variables? Ignoring a variable doesn't mean it isn't present, of course. Even if a particular study were to include only middle-class standard-English speakers, standard English in Cambridge, Massachusetts has a different phonology from that in Athens, Georgia or Manning, Alberta.

In fact, since many of the studies Adams cites compare low and high achievers and readers with varying amounts of economic advantage, the researchers had to be ignoring — or were ignorant of — socio-economic dialect differences that existed among their subjects. Often these research reports contain subtle forms of elitism and racism in the very research models they employ. Yet often the biased results are used to justify direct instruction in phonics for minority students.

Here is one of many examples from Adams:

"... productive phonic instruction is far less tricky for students who enter school with solid literacy preparation ... for well-prepared children, such instruction consists as much of review and clarification as it does of new content.

"... To gain proper registration, phonic instruction must articulate with the understanding and expectations of the learners. ... Many children enter first grade prepared with much of the understanding, expectations and prior knowledge required by their lessons. ...

"Other children begin first grade without such preparation. In the extreme, these children will come to know only what we have helped them to learn and only as we have helped them to learn it." (pp. 291-292)

But "to gain proper registration," phonic instruction must articulate with the oral dialect of the learners. Poor children tend to come from groups that speak low-status dialects, and when they don't respond to biased phonics instruction, teachers conclude that they lack "solid literacy preparation."

Reductionist researchers ignore dialect differences, as well as many other characteristics of their subjects' language, in their research. But then they use the biased findings to arrive at universal instructional prescriptions: all children must be taught what other kids have learned and that includes phonics. According to Adams and her colleagues, the groups they've misrepresented and misunderstood in their studies are precisely the ones who need prescribed and controlled — and dialect inappropriate — phonics instruction.

Adams doesn't altogether ignore "outside-in models of reading" — a put-down term for models that give importance to what the reader brings to the reading. Here's her version of my model of reading:

> "It might be argued that the processes that skilled readers use in recognizing isolated words are not necessarily the same as those they will use in reading coherent text. In particular a major difference between skillful readers and beginners is that skillful readers possess a vast, overlearned repertoire of knowledge about written text — not just about spelling but also about the syntax and semantics of language and about the normal flow of discourse. It seems an irresistible hypothesis that the reader might somehow use this information to guide and, thereby, reduce the visual work involved in reading meaningful, connected text.
>
> ". . . In particular, skilled readers might use their predictions to guide their visual inspection of the text. They might skip, skim, or pore over individual letters only as necessary to confirm or correct their expectations as to its message." (p. 99)

What follows this quote is a very careful summary of the literature on eye movements (to judge whether readers anticipate what they see) and "semantic preprocessing" (to judge whether readers anticipate meaning). That review leads her to the conclusion that ". . . mature readers do not recognize words holistically, even though that's what they look like they do" and "mature readers do not use context to help them recognize words, even though that's what they feel like they do." (p. 103)

Miscue research, as my earlier examples showed, has demonstrated that all readers, not just mature readers, have control over the "syntax and semantics of language and . . . the normal flow of discourse." They couldn't speak or understand speech otherwise. Remember how Patricia did "skip, skim, or pore over individual letters"? (See pp. 57-59.) Yet she had variable success as she swung between making sense of the text and trying to use all of the letters to get the words right.

What children *learn* as they read is how all three information systems operate together in written language. They *already know* how to make sense of oral language. Like Patricia, they *can be taught* to do things in reading that get in the way of making sense.

Note that while Adams starts out examining a view she says deals with the difference between recognizing words and reading coherent text, she tests that view with studies of word recognition. Furthermore, she takes into consideration none of the miscue and other psycholinguistic research that led to the theory she's examining. Although she's generally very thorough in citing research, these studies apparently don't exist for her, perhaps because they don't fit within her paradigm. She sees a socio-psycholinguist theory as an "outside-in" theory without a research base capable of being tested in the "instructional and laboratory arenas."

At the same time, she does credit us with a theory and a few interesting ideas for teachers:

> ". . . the Goodmans . . . have translated their theory into some excellent recommendations and activities toward developing children's appreciation of text and thoughtfulness during reading." (p. 99)

but her bottom line remains firm:

> ". . . If we could release children from letterwise processing of text, we could expedite their graduation into efficient, skillful readers. Yet the single immutable and nonoptional fact about skillful reading is that it involves relatively complete processing of the individual letters of print." (p. 105)

Rather than simply stating how wrong I believe this "nonoptional fact" to be, I'm going to let you demonstrate that to yourself through the following simple experiment. It's one I've used for years, and was the subject of a doctoral study by Fred Gollasch (1980).

> Directions: *Read the the text that follows though once, and once only. Don't go back during the reading or reread at the end. When your done turn the book over and write everything you remember reading.*

The Boat in the Basement

A woman was building a boat in
her basement. When she had finished the
the boot, she discovered that it was
too big to go though the door. So he
had to take the boat a part to get
it out. She should of planned ahead.

I hope you followed my instructions and didn't cheat, but from my experience I suspect that some of you did. You knew you weren't supposed to go back during your reading but you did it anyway. Others wanted to, but were dutiful and resisted the impulse.

Now take a look at what you wrote. My instruction to you was "write everything you remember reading." Did you reproduce the font of the book in your writing? Not likely. You wrote in the normal handwriting you usually use, cursive or manuscript, and the result didn't look much like the text. You must have interpreted my "remember reading" to mean comprehending. You produced the message but not the exact letter forms. That's no small matter; *you remembered what you perceived and understood, not what you saw.*

What you wrote isn't likely to be a verbatim match of the words in the text either. You retold the story but not in the same words. You might find it interesting to examine the changes you made. In Australia, for example, where they don't have many basements, some readers wrote about a *garage*.

But so far we haven't proved Adams' *non-optional fact* to be wrong. She could argue that you did recognize each letter and word and simply transformed them in the writing task. So now let me explain the design of the Gollasch study, a real experiment even by her standards.

He used four groups: a group of seventh graders and one of university juniors, each divided in half. One half of each main group was given the instructions I gave you; the others were told that the text they would be given had errors in it, and they were to read to find those errors. After the reading, they were all asked to write what they remembered reading and list any errors they had detected in the text. We expected that the groups invited to read for errors would find more than those that weren't told there were errors present. We also assumed that looking for errors might interfere with comprehension, so those retellings would be less successful. And we assumed that we'd find big differences between seventh grade and university students.

Here are Gollasch's results:

➤ The "error" groups found more of the errors. Though the difference was statistically significant (because the N was sufficiently large) it was not a big difference. The "error" groups found slightly more than three on the average, the others slightly fewer than three. (How many did you notice?)

➤ The college folks found more errors than the seventh graders. Again the difference was significant but not great, and again centered on three.

➤ They all got the meaning — telling them to look for errors didn't deter them from making sense of the text. That was as true for the seventh graders as it was for the college students.

➤ Even when they had unlimited time to find the errors, virtually none of the subjects found all six. (Feel better now?)

Let's consider the errors that were deliberately inserted into this passage in the order in which they're most likely to be detected, according to the research.

➤ *Boot* for *boat* on line 3. Most subjects noticed this. It's also the place where most people feel compelled to reread. Their predictions are contradicted, so they reread to get more information. If you didn't detect this you probably wrote *boat* throughout your retelling. You may have detected *boot* but wrote *boat* anyway, dismissing it as a typo. A few people assume that some part of a *boat* is called the *boot*, as the British call the trunk of a car the *boot*.

➤ *He* for *she* in line 4. Surprisingly, the majority caught this one as well. Again it seems to be a conflict in information that causes people to be brought up short by the appearance of *he*, even though it looks a lot like *she*. These two errors are most centrally related to making sense of the story.

➤ *A part* for *apart* in line 5. Considerably fewer people notice this, usually about half in my audiences. The issue here is not in the letters but in whether a word or a noun phrase belongs in this context.

➤ *Should of* for *should've* in line 6. In my presentations I usually play a game in discussing this error. I say, "It should've been what?" Usually someone responds "should have." *Should've* is a well accepted contraction, *should of* a common misspelling of the contraction. I'm saying misspelling because it's grammatically impossible for *of* to follow *should* in English grammar. Very few of either the seventh graders or the college students caught this error. We'd expected more difference, because about 1 in 5 teachers in my audiences catch it. This is similar to spelling *you're* as *your* — which I did just for fun in the directions for this experiment. Did you notice?

➤ *Though* for *through* in line 4. Almost no one catches this. It's a good example of how selective perception is in reading. We know that *ough* is not very useful in telling words apart or predicting their pronunciation, so we pay little attention to it. By the time readers reach this point in the text they are predicting very strongly where the text is going. They expect to see *through* and get enough confirmation to be satisfied, since nothing subsequent causes any disconfirmation.

➤ An extra *the* at the end of line 2. A whole extra word is the hardest to detect, even when you're looking for errors. The human brain acts intelligently. It uses its sensors — the eyes, for example — to gather sensory, visual information. But it reserves for itself the task of making sense of this, and it constructs its perceptions on the basis of what it expects. It isn't that the eye doesn't see *the the*. The brain only perceives one because two are not possible. Making sense is the brain's active priority. Does it first see and then perceive? Not exactly. It knows what it's looking for and uses all it knows about language to select what it needs to for forming perceptions and making sense. What's important in perception is what we expect to see and what we think we are seeing.

So let me summarize. Perception in reading is a very efficient process. The brain, the organ of human intelligence, is engaged in far more than recognizing known entities. It actively seeks meaning. It controls the sensory organs and uses them to select and sample from available input, print in the case of reading.

There's no reason for an efficient and effective reader to notice any of these deliberate errors. The fact that we do notice some of them has to do with the tentativeness and self-monitoring that characterizes reading. We keep checking ourselves, and sometimes we catch things that don't matter much. Important things like *boot* for *boat* or *he* for *she* get caught because they disrupt our expectations of the meaning. Self-correction of miscues that affect meaning turned out to be one of the most important aspects of reading in our miscue research and in Marie Clay's study in New Zealand. (Clay, 1979)

By the way, there were two more deliberate errors in the directions for the experiment. Did you notice them too? If you didn't catch the three errors, did you comprehend the instructions anyway? No, says Adams. Yes, say I. What say you?

This, then, I would like to say to Adams: not only can we liberate children from letter-by-letter processing of a text, but also we can avoid enslaving them in such an unnatural process in the first place — and that should be our priority as teachers.

As I said, we're engaged here in the politics of research paradigms. Hers is a paradigm of instructional and laboratory studies; mine is a paradigm of the real world of reading. In her paradigm she can ignore my research since she has no place to put it; in my paradigm I must deal with her research and put it in the real world. And the real world of reading is making sense of print, not recognizing words.

8

*Some people
further their own
political purposes by
using phonics to frighten
and politicize rural and
working-class
parents.*

The politics of phonics

If the phonics instruction case represented by Adams is so clearly not a representation of how accomplished language practioners got to be that way, then why is there so much public to-do about the subject?

In this chapter I want to add more examples of the public politics of phonics to those I included at the beginning of the book, and show that, especially in the United States, much of the current furor has political rather than educational, scholarly or scientific motivations.

The Reading Reform Foundation is a US-based group, though active in other countries as well, that is dedicated to what they call "Systematic Intensive Phonics." In its *Basic Information and Catalog*, the RRF includes an article called "The Epidemic of Reading Disabilities," by Dr. Carl Kline and Carolyn Lacey Kline, from Canada:

"When 35% of the population is affected by a disability, it is an epidemic. When that disability is the leading cause of emotional problems in children and adolescents in North America, we are talking about a serious public health problem. Consider also that this epidemic is a major etiological factor in school-dropouts and in juvenile delinquency. Furthermore . . . it seems likely that teenagers who can't read or spell and who consequently hate school are easy targets for drug dealers.

"We already have the vaccine to attack reading disability, but we can't get the educators to use it. Samuel Orton, Rudolf Flesch, Jeanne Chall,

Patrick Groff and numerous other researchers have urged the educators to prevent this massive problem by inoculating primary students with a steady injection of synthetic, explicit phonics." (p. 6)

The form and content of this and similar media items are often revealing, particularly in their use of simplistic logic. In this case it's dressed up in a medical metaphor:

➤ Huge numbers of people aren't learning to read.

➤ That produces many other problems: emotional problems, school drop-outs, delinquency and drug use.

➤ All that could easily be avoided with a shot of synthetic, explicit phonics.

➤ Teachers and others who don't agree are part of a conspiracy to deprive children of literacy and destroy the fibre of society.

I'm sure that some of the people who believe this simplistic logic are utterly sincere. Parents worried about their own children and apprehensive about the recent economic, political and social upheavals around the world turn their attention to schools and schooling as remedies against further unrest and uncertainty.

The January 12, 1993, edition of *The Globe and Mail* mentions several parent groups that have recently sprung up in Canada. There are, for example: Parents Against Reduction in Education [Quality] Networking Together (Nova Scotia), Reading and Literacy Institute (Alberta), Parents for Basics (Manitoba), Quality Education Network (Ontario) and Concerned Adults for Responsible Education (British Columbia). While these groups aren't necessarily agreed on all concerns, the term "basics" as a code word for "phonics-first instruction" crops up regularly.

Parents have a right, even a duty, to be concerned about the educational welfare of their children, but in most cases competent and thoughtful teachers are well able to provide reassuring answers about the language education their children are receiving.

However, especially in the United States, others are using phonics as a means of furthering their political agendas, as a means of frightening and politicizing especially rural and working-class parents. They use phonics-first campaigns to be elected as local school board members, to lobby for state "choice" and voucher programs, and even to influence federal policies and laws.

Charlotte T. Iserbyt's article "Reading Is the Civil Rights Issue of the 90's" was read into the Congressional Record of October 23, 1989 by congressman Joseph E. Brennan. In another version of the same article, which appeared in the March, 1990 issue of the *AFA Journal*, Iserbyt said:

"Why don't our media education moguls, who seem almost to delight in parading uneducated American public school students across our TV screens for all the world to see, ever discuss the real cause of illiteracy: the use of whole-language/look-say reading instruction?

"A wall of silence, as potentially deadly as the Berlin Wall (if you cannot read, you are not free) has been erected, blocking out the views of pro-intensive phonics educators.

"Dr. Kenneth Lexier, former Assistant Superintendent in a large school district in Maine, says, 'the almost total avoidance of the research supporting a code emphasis [intensive phonics] in beginning reading instruction may be one of the most outrageous injustices perpetuated by our preservice training institutions. From small state colleges to major universities, the bias is clear and undeniable — phonics is out and whole language is in . . . This is a conspiracy worthy of a Washington Post expose.'" (p. 18, deletions hers)

Again the view is simplistic: phonics is truth, all else is a conspiracy of lies. Approaches like this make it hard to shed light on phonics and reading instruction.

The terminology being employed in these political debates creates continuous confusion, at times deliberate, between *research* (studies of reading as a process including phonics) and *programs* (for instruction of reading focused on phonics). In the US Senate Republican Policy Committee document "Illiteracy: An Incurable Disease or Education Malpractice?" the politicalization of phonics is made very clear, while the issues of reading process and instruction are hopelessly muddled:

"Based on a 1987 study by the U.S. Department of Education, *Preventing Reading Failure: The Myths of Reading Instruction* [Groff], 90% of remedial reading students today are not able to decode fluently, accurately, and at an automatic level of response. In a March, 1989 *Phi Delta Kappan* article, Harvard Professor Jeanne Chall (author of *Learning to Read, The Great Debate*, 1983) cites a study by Peter Freebody and Brian Byrne that confirms the same finding. Today's students are not being taught the fundamental structure of language, but rather are engaged in what Dr. Kenneth Goodman (a proponent of 'the whole language approach') has called a 'psycholinguistic guessing game.'" (p. 3)

I don't disagree that readers are engaged in a "psycholinguistic guessing game" — that's reading. But the implication here is that that's what students have been taught to do instead of phonics and, had they been taught phonics, they would be "able to decode fluently, accurately, and at an automatic level of response." *Decode,* as it's used here, means to match letters and sounds. But I call that *recoding,* since the sounds still have to be decoded to get to meaning. Think about an army signal corps operator who gets a message in dots and dashes, recodes those as letters and only then decodes to meaning.

The document refers more positively to Jeanne Chall, the academic source most cited both to prove the effectiveness of phonics and to support the truth vs. lies, phonics vs. everything view. Here are examples from her own writing:

> "I did a synthesis in 1967 and updated it in 1983 . . . and found systematic phonics (learning the alphabetic principle) along with the reading of stories to be superior to the so-called natural approaches (whole word, sight, whole language) — which propose story reading only . . ." (syndicated column, 1991)

> ". . . whole language instruction — the current meaning-emphasis approach to beginning reading — tends to be associated with a natural, 'developmental' and open view. It is further assumed by many that 'open', 'natural' reading programs that do not teach directly lead to greater cognitive development and to greater love of reading and learning, although there is little evidence to support these claims." (*Phi Delta Kappan,* March, 1989, p. 530)

> "It's not that whole language does not have research evidence — and it does not — but they are deliberately turning their backs on the existing solid research that exists for the opposite . . .

> ". . . we've been getting into our reading lab more children who need help in 1st or 2nd grade. Twenty years ago, we did not get any until 3rd or 4th grade . . . they are beginning to fall off in 1st grade, and they come from areas where they teach whole language, not skills." (*Education Week,* March 21, 1990, p. 10)

Chall has, in fact, not studied phonics. Her research has dealt with looking at the results of other people's instructional studies that claimed to use direct "systematic" phonics as the principal means of reading instruction in contrast with other methods she first called "meaning emphasis" and now calls "natural" or "story-reading only."

The Senate document continues:

> "In December of 1982, a survey of 1609 professors of reading in 300 graduate schools was conducted. When asked which reading authorities of all time, in their opinion, had written the most significant, most worthy, 'classic' studies in reading, the top three individuals on the list, in order, were Frank Smith, Kenneth Goodman, and Edmund Huey, all well-known,

vociferous, dedicated, dogmatic, (sic) enemies of early, intensive teaching
of phonics. Frank Smith and Kenneth Goodman are two of today's most
influential proponents of the 'look and say' or, as they would term it,
'whole language' method of teaching reading." (pp. 7-8)

And Edmund Huey has been dead for almost a century! Notice again the
confusion of terms in this political game: "look and say" . . . "whole language." If
it's not phonics, it doesn't matter what it's called. It's all the same.

And here is the medical diagnosis again:

"The overwhelming evidence from research and classroom results indicates
that the cure for the 'disease of illiteracy' is the restoration of the
instructional practice of intensive, systematic phonics in every primary
school in America!" (p. 13)

Mighty leaps of logic are common in the documents and speeches of those
who push the politics of phonics-first instruction. The conclusion here is that
those who are illiterate are so because they didn't get intensive systematic
phonics instruction as all primary school pupils did at some unspecified former
time. (I'll come back to that issue in the next chapter.)

My final quotation comes from one who seems so intent on "winning" the
politics of phonics-first instruction that no boundaries of civility in language or
accuracy in fact exist anymore:

"We can expect the whole language fanatics to do everything in their
power to discredit intensive phonics with their usual lies and
misrepresentations. Although the new studies are needed to counter the
'studies' concocted by the charlatans of whole language, we have 4000
years of experience in teaching children to read an alphabetic writing
system to draw upon. Ken Goodman talks of 'current cognitive research' as
if those 4000 years of teaching experience never took place.

"Obviously, whole language is not a method of teaching children to
read. It is a political program with the goal of turning American children
into little socialists." (*Blumenfeld Education Letter*, February 1992, p. 6)

I'll leave you to draw your own conclusions about "lies and
misrepresentations." I'll just say this: it seems clear to me that these comments
aren't about phonics, illiteracy or "4000 years of teaching experience" at all.
They're about the political aspirations of a phonics-first lobby.

Unfortunately, the interests of that lobby have merged with the interest of
some reading researchers. Let's see how.

The politics of research

The basic "findings" of the Adams report were determined in advance by a government agency.

In 1975 Richard Anderson, a research psychologist at the University of Illinois, won a grant from the US National Institute of Education to begin the Center for the Study of Reading. Bolt, Beranek and Newman, a private, profit-making research group in Cambridge, Massachusetts, listed on the New York Stock Exchange, was co-grantee. In keeping with its commitment to free enterprise, the US government does not limit competitions for research support to non-profit agencies.

Anderson's team was primarily interested in reading comprehension. The participants had a common interest in schema theory as a means of explaining comprehension, and little interest in reading instruction, particularly in beginning readers. When the book *Becoming a Nation of Readers* emerged from the Center in 1985, however, the phonics-first lobby was happy; it greeted this report as a total vindication of its position. Newspaper editorials proclaimed that the Center had proved phonics to be the method of choice. *Readers Digest* and the Reading Reform Foundation ran a full-page ad in the *New York Times* announcing the victory. The report was sold by professional organizations, and annotated copies were distributed free by basal publishers.

But the phonics-first lobby wanted more than a justification of its position, it also wanted Washington to pass federal laws mandating phonics in reading instruction and teacher education. It went even further, calling for a listing of the most "cost effective" phonics programs. And those pressures succeeded in making the production of a new phonics report an explicit condition for continued government funding of the Center.

So Anderson's attempt to avoid getting caught in the politics of phonics by issuing an endorsement of it only got him further into it. According to Pearson in the foreword to the later Adams' report, "it was *Becoming a Nation of Readers* . . . that spawned the legislation (authored by the late senator Zorinsky of Nebraska) commissioning this report on phonics."

Marilyn Adams, a psychological researcher at Bolt, Beranek and Newman, was commissioned by the Center to do the second report. This chain of events brought the phonics-first lobby — whose heroes within education included Jeanne Chall, Patrick Groff and Jay Samuels — into a new relationship with a major group of reading researchers. Never before had any research center or researcher accepted a direct commission to marshall the research literature in support of phonics and its political advocates. The "findings" of the Adams report were determined in advance by a federal government agency acting on instructions from Congress. And the sponsor found the report acceptable. (Senator Zorinsky died in the interim.)

Within a few days of the release of Adams' book, Senator Armstrong said this on the floor of the Senate:

> "In a major new study on reading instruction released in January, 1990 entitled *Beginning to Read, Thinking and Learning about Print*, Marilyn J. Adams, a researcher at Bolt, Beranek and Newman Inc. in Cambridge, MA, recognizes phonics as an essential ingredient of early reading instruction. She concludes that: 'Research indicates that to become proficient readers, children need to learn and be able to use the relationships between letters and sounds and that explicit instruction of these relationships leads to improved reading achievement.'" (Armstrong, 1990)

Ironically, while there is much in Adams' report to give solace to the phonics-first lobby, the close reading we did in the preceding chapter also revealed some basic anomalies between the lobby position and Adams'. Although she's not exactly advocating the mythical "look-say" view that Rudolph Flesch conjured up as the opposite of phonics programs, she does advocate a *look-recognition* model. And in the long run that can't be entirely pleasing to the ultimate sponsors of the book, the phonics-first lobby.

What can we do about the politics of phonics? In the final chapter of this book I first want to answer some of the claims made by the phonics-first lobby. Then I'll briefly present my own case for phonics in reading instruction.

9

*Today
more children
are learning to read and
write through authentic
book experiences
and literacy
events.*

Phonics in reading instruction

Senator Armstrong, quoted earlier, has a lot of the history wrong. Most of us were not taught to read through a method called phonics. We were taught to read with basal readers filled with controlled vocabulary and "word attack skills," including phonics.

In fact there never was a period when most learners where taught exclusively with a "phonics" method. And there was no sharp, pervasive change 20 years ago in the way reading was taught in North America. Since the early 1930s, basal readers have dominated American reading instruction. In fact, in the 1970s, a strong back-to-basics movement successfully pushed for heavier explicit instruction in phonics in the basals.

Only in the last decade has there been a definite shift away from basals towards whole language and the use of real children's literature in reading programs (the two overlap but are not the same). And basals have responded by including more real literature, less heavily edited. That's just to get the facts right.

There is no evidence of any "disastrous consequences" to literacy beginning 20 years ago. On the contrary, the shift toward whole language programs and the use of real literature has pushed sales of children's books up 500% in the last 10 years. The use of children's rooms in libraries is up dramatically. A lot of children are reading a lot more. And more children are learning to read and write through authentic whole language experiences. Those are also facts, easy to verify.

Which gets us to the issue of phonics as a method of teaching reading. People keep reinventing phonics as a simple, easy way to teach kids to read. *Hooked on Phonics*, an audio-tape based phonics program heavily promoted on radio and television, is just one of these simplistic inventions. It is promoted as a complete program for teaching beginners, remedial readers and adult illiterates. Its claims are so extravagant that it's actually been repudiated by a wide range of professional authorities, including an International Reading Association task force that included Jeanne Chall.

Its premise, like that of all such programs, is the "common sense" notion that if people learn to match a small number of letters and a small number of sounds, they can read. That leads to the simplistic conclusion that if they don't learn to read it's because they haven't been taught phonics. This simplistic reasoning then leads to the notion that, since all this is so obvious, there must be a conspiracy to keep people from being taught this sure, simple way.

But, as I've shown, the phonic relationships in English, or any alphabetically written languages, are anything but simple. Furthermore, and here's an even more serious problem, these relationships are abstract: when we deal with phonics, we're dealing not with the relationship of language to meaning or to things, we're dealing with relationships between two abstract systems, oral and written language.

Phonics-first reading programs are based on the most simplistic version of the phonics instruction argument. They focus entirely on teaching phonics *prior* to any other instruction or experience with reading. Learners must survive an extended teaching of letter-sound correspondences before they are permitted to experience anything like meaningful language. And that's bad phonics. It's bad because it's oversimplified, inaccurate, out of context and inappropriate for the learners. Although they don't address the inaccurate phonics typical of these programs, both Anderson and Adams recognize that they are essentially incomplete and unlikely to be successful. And still both repeatedly indicate their belief in the validity of research showing such programs to be successful!

Anderson says:

"In an excess of zeal to get phonics across, some programs introduce the sounds of many letters before providing opportunities to use what has been learned in reading words in sentences and stories." (p. 42)

Adams says:

". . . Assuming the teaching of two or three correspondences per week and even assuming perfect learning, it would take many years to cover all possible spelling-sound translations. Without the rewards of reading, what child would sit still for such instruction?" (p. 272)

Both agree that teaching phonics is insufficient to make readers of non-readers. That leaves them with a dilemma: how can children learn the phonics they supposedly need in order to read and still get into reading early enough to keep interested in learning?

The basal reading series solution is to start the children reading simplified controlled vocabulary stories, at the same time teaching phonics as part of a skill sequence. Not surprisingly, the stories never contain only words that use the phonic relationships already taught. Partly that's because of those factors I've mentioned that complicate phonics relationships, and partly because telling a story can't be done while controlling phonic relationships. Some of the most common words in English don't fit into common phonic patterns. Where attempts are made to stay with words that do fit phonic patterns, the results are alliterative tongue-twisters that are in no sense believable narratives.

If there is research that claims that phonics-first or hybrid basal phonics programs "work," it's because tests used to measure reading achievement include items and sub-tests, particularly at the early levels, that are very much like the workbook pages the children have experienced in their instruction. The children are being judged on their success with the phonics drills, not on their success in making sense of print.

If children come to read and write through these programs, it's not because of the programs, but because of the ability of most children to learn language, including reading and writing, in spite of obstacles put in their way. Fortunately, no one has yet been able to devise an instructional program so bad that it has succeeded in keeping the majority of pupils from learning.

I considered providing some examples at this point to show how unscientific, inaccurate and misleading much of the phonics instruction in current instructional programs is — there is certainly no shortage of examples. But I decided not to waste time and space. I've given you some understanding of English phonics. Check the phonics instruction out for yourself to see how bad it is. You'll look in vain for any sensitivity to dialect differences. You'll find no concern for variations in fonts. And you'll find a good deal of "linguistic science fiction": misinformation in the name of teaching phonics.

Fortunately, we now understand how phonics works in productive reading and writing, as one among several sources of information available to readers and writers as they read and write. And we understand how readers and writers come to control the complexities of orthography and phonics as they learn to make sense through written language. Because learners are trying to make sense as they learn to use phonics and all the available information, they learn to be selective, to know how much of each kind of information is needed at any given point.

Effective, efficient reading is not rapid, automatic word recognition. It's constructing meaning with the least amount of effort and energy. Kids learn to control phonics much more easily than Adams and Anderson give them credit for, when they encounter authentic and meaningful texts. The task becomes hard only when we try to isolate phonics relationships and teach them directly.

Phonics in whole language

Whole language teachers don't reject phonics; what they do is put it in its proper place.

If we don't need "direct" instruction that focuses on distorted, hard-to-learn, out-of-context phonics, what do we need? We need instruction that supports the learning that children are naturally engaged in as they try to make sense of written language.

Whole language is the term given to instructional curriculum that builds on the view that readers and writers integrate all available information in authentic literacy events as they make sense of print. Whole language teachers don't reject phonics; they put it in its proper place. They understand that in learning to read and write an alphabetic language, hearing pupils *will* come to understand the alphabetic system and *will* invent ways of relating their own speech to print, whatever the dialect.

Kid-watching whole language teachers know how to spot the movement of learners toward controlling the use of all available cue systems while they are making sense of print. They see the evidence in the invented spellings of young writers and in the miscues of young readers. That's why they know that the best way to teach children to read and write is to immerse them in reading and writing from the very beginning. They accept the kids' scribbles and watch with interest as those scribbles become strings of letters, then representations of words and syllables, and then comprehensible invented spellings.

They turn their classrooms into rich literate environments. And all along the way they provide many invitations and opportunities for the children to play at writing and to write for authentic purposes. They note how children move from knowing that print in the environment has meaning, to holistically remembering favorite books, to knowing how print makes sense. Their pupils are always involved in functional reading and writing.

This book isn't about whole language teaching, however, and I won't provide here the details of how whole language teachers develop readers and writers — that book is to come. All I need to say here is that whole language values phonics in literacy development to the extent — and only to the extent — that it is part of making sense of print.

Not only does whole language teaching value phonics; it is, in fact, the only instruction that includes a scientific understanding of the nature of phonics and the way the very complex phonic relationships are learned. Since children can learn phonics only in the context of reading and writing, whole language teachers monitor their students' development. They watch for the signs in Shoshana's writing and in Patricia's reading that tell where they are in their development and what kinds of support and help they need. Knowledgeable teachers give enough support to build on the children's strengths and help them over their hangups and plateaus. Patricia needs to be encouraged to take more risks and trust herself to make sense of print. Shoshana needs to be encouraged to check her inventions against her developing sense of spelling conventions as she prepares her writing for publication.

Too often we think of teaching as telling kids what they need to know and then making them practice until they know it. Since that works, in a measurable sense, only on very finite tasks, we chop complex learning into a series of bite-size bits and teach and test each bit as an end in itself. Phonics programs have been like that. But really effective teaching is finding out what learners are doing and helping them do it. Whole language teachers support the control of the phonics system their pupils develop as they try to make sense.

What we've learned from the study of language development, both oral and written, is that language is easy to learn when we deal with the whole of it as we use it functionally to make sense. Little children are understanding and making themselves understood in oral language long before they fully control the sound system. That's because they learn language in the context of its use. Children learn written language in the same way. They may learn the names of letters as they're learning to read, and even have some sense of how they relate to sounds. But they can learn the abstract phonics systems only in the context of trying to make sense of meaningful print. They're very good at learning language when it's in authentic, meaningful context. They're not very good at learning abstractions out of context.

Current research shows very young children becoming aware of the alphabetic nature of written English. They invent spellings as they experiment with writing and are able to test out their own developing phonics rules. These invented phonics rules often show the keen hearing of young learners. They hear features adults have learned to ignore. Gradually they, too, begin to tune out features that aren't important in the system. At the same time they learn the limitations of phonics rules for producing correct spellings.

Building a set for diversity

I've built a case for the need for readers and writers to deal with a wide range of fonts and a wide range of spellings that can't be predicted from a set of rules. We should be grateful that the strong advocates of direct instruction haven't understood this diversity. If they had, they'd be teaching each font, each minor rule, each of the myriad of unique spellings.

Actually, children learn to deal with this diversity in written language much as they learn to deal with the diversity of oral language. Voices are certainly as unique as handwriting, for example, yet children learn to perceive the significant features of the language sounds while learning to ignore other differences. If they heard only one voice, they couldn't build this set for diversity.

Only if children encounter a diversity of fonts in their reading can they develop a sense of diversity in writing. Fortunately, they already encounter this diversity in the real world. Environmental print is marvelously diverse. It tends toward capital letters, which is why many children start writing their names and other attempts at writing in capitals. Because the shift from manuscript to cursive writing in school is abrupt, there's a brief period when many children have difficulty producing and reading cursive writing, but this is short-lived.

Children's ability to deal with diversity is truly amazing:

➤ They are able to internalize variable distinctive features and treat very different allographs as the same graphemes, the same perceived letter units.

➤ They have no trouble developing the schwa rule, unless a teacher insists on the stressed form in all cases, or unless words are taught in isolation so the vowels are always stressed.

➤ They invent phonics rules for relating their own dialect to English spelling, and learn the unique spellings of words in their authentic, holistic reading and writing.

But *why* are we surprised, after all, by young children's ability to deal with diversity? They've been doing it for a long time — in calling very different looking animals dogs, for instance, and not confusing them with cats or teddybears. Diversity is a characteristic of human language, and problems in dealing with that diversity aren't likely to occur unless well-meaning teachers or instructional program writers make it a problem.

Phonics and reading difficulties

The school tends to blame the students when it's really the school that fails.

Many reading difficulties are made worse rather than better by well-meaning but misconceived instruction.

While there is no epidemic of dyslexia in any literate country, there are certainly some children who have difficulty learning to read. Indications from a variety of sources show that more of these children are found among the poor, ethnic and linguistic minorities, and also males. This uneven distribution may well reflect the relative inability of the pupils to adjust to the expectations of the schools, and the relative inflexibility of the schools in adjusting to the learners.

Schools tend to blame the pupils for any school failure. So instead of building on the strengths of the learners, particularly their ability to learn language in meaningful, functional contexts, the schools remediate them with increased doses of out-of-context phonics and word-attack skills. Ironically, in skill-based and phonics-first programs, Patricia's overuse of phonics is interpreted as proof that she needs more phonics instruction. The result is a self-fulfilling prophesy: the pupils become discouraged and convinced that they're incapable of becoming literate, and the more they fail, the more abstract, decontextualized practice they are given.

Too much out-of-context and uninformed phonics can produce problems for precisely those children who are less likely to succeed in our schools. They are made to believe that reading is word recognition, so they think that if they can't recognize words immediately, or sound them out, they can never become literate. They become their own worst enemies as they accept the blame for their lack of success. These are children who need to find reading and writing as relevant, as useful and as interesting as oral language. They need to be involved in using real reading and real writing for their own functional needs.

Among very young beginners there are children who haven't even discovered that English writing is alphabetic. But the work of Yetta Goodman, Emilia Ferreiro and many others demonstrates that children learn first that writing is a way of making sense. As they come to understand that, they then also come to understand *how* writing systems are used to make sense. Teachers can support this learning by involving beginners in authentic reading and writing and helping their pupils to see the part-whole relationships in their reading and writing.

The appropriate instruction for learners-in-trouble, therefore, is to help them begin to revalue themselves as learners, and to revalue the process of reading and writing as making sense of print.

My experience is that most uncertain pupils have all the necessary strategies, but they lack confidence in their ability to use them. Like Patricia, they fall back on phonics because they've come to believe any other strategy is cheating. Usually just supporting them as they read meaningful, interesting material, encouraging them to take risks and trust themselves, and reminding them it's all supposed to make sense, is enough to help them out of the rut they've been pushed into.

Older pupils and adults who have long histories of unsuccessful attempts at becoming literate in school are particularly prone to blame themselves for their failures. They need great patience from supportive teachers. They need to revalue their ways of coping with print in the environment, in their life and work. Retrospective miscue analysis — having them record their own oral reading and then talk through their miscues with a teacher and/or one or more peers — is a very effective way to help such readers revalue themselves and the process.

Very often the first breakthrough comes in writing, because the remedial programs they've been used to have so focused on reading skills that they've never been asked to write. Their early writing will no doubt include many invented spellings, showing that they don't lack phonic insights. But they'll move more quickly toward social conventions than young children, particularly if they are also beginning to read more freely.

Appropriate instructional materials

For generations teachers have known intuitively that the best way for children to learn to read and write is by reading and writing. Yet they permitted themselves to be persuaded that children must first be made "ready" for real reading and writing through an increasing array of "readiness" materials.

These materials were based on the unexamined principle that children must learn parts before wholes. The effect they often had was to make the children, already on their way to reading and writing before they came to school, doubt themselves and become confused about themselves as learners. And the teachers took this lack of success and confusion as proof that they needed the readiness materials.

Immense instructional programs (basal readers) were developed to control the skills pupils must learn before they could be trusted to make sense of print. The stories in the basals were organized to give practice in the words and skills that were specifically and sequentially introduced, and this instructional technology became the reading curriculum. Progress through the pre-primers, primers and graded texts was equated with learning to read. And both teachers and learners came to think that reading the stories in the textbooks was less important than completing the workbook exercises and skill drills.

The stories in the basals, even those taken from real children's literature, were rewritten and censored to make them conform to the scope and sequences laid down in the programs. Not only were they refocused, without thought to literary integrity, on the words and skills being introduced, they were also censored to make sure they didn't offend any special interest groups.

There's been widespread rebellion against these highly controlled and artificial materials, however. California's criteria for state adoption have led the way in requiring publishers to use real and unedited literature. And the whole language movement has led to the abandonment of basals in favor of a program based entirely on pupils reading real books in a wide range of genres and integrated with the rest of the curriculum. In this process, the thoughtful and inventive work of Canadian, Australian and New Zealand educators have become an inspiration for American teachers.

Writing in the elementary school and even in secondary schools had been reduced to component mechanics: handwriting, spelling and grammar. The process writing movement that has taken place throughout the English-speaking world, the national writing project in the United States, and the whole language movement in general have given writing a new status in the curriculum.

All this means that many children are doing authentic reading and writing right from the time they enter school. Both teachers and children have been liberated from the basal technology, enabling the children to invent their own phonics systems as they learn to make sense through written language. They invent spelling and punctuation as they write because they have something to say. Their teachers help them to discover conventions and to bring their inventions ever closer to equilibrium with the conventions. That's a fancy way of saying that they become more conventional as they become more and more confident and effective in their reading and writing, but not at the expense of their creativity.

A whole new genre of children's literature has emerged: predictable books. The concept of predictability comes out of the psycholinguistic research that established prediction as an important strategy in making sense of print. Texts are harder or easier to read depending on how predictable they are for particular readers. What makes a text predictable is the extent to which it fits the reader's knowledge, interests and language competence. For beginners with limited experience in reading, highly predictable books are comprehensible and build their developing strategies, including the graphophonic strategies. As with oral language development, children make sense of the system of language as they make sense of the language event, the literacy event.

Predictability is a factor at all stages of reading development. It also helps with second-language development. If readers find texts interesting and useful to themselves, they can usually succeed in comprehending them, while at the same time learning the English vocabulary and orthography.

Building the school literacy program around authentic, holistic and functional reading and writing doesn't neglect phonics, spelling, the mechanics of writing or any of the other traditional concerns of language arts instruction. It simply puts them in proper perspective and creates the optimal conditions for their development. Teachers, as perceptive kid-watchers, continually monitor and support this development.

The place for phonics

Though phonics is an intrinsic part of reading English, when we make phonics a method of teaching reading by teaching letter-sound relationships out of context, we're making these mistakes:

➤ We're turning reading from a process of making sense into one of saying sounds for letters.

➤ We're ignoring what kids already know about how to make sense of print.

➤ We're ignoring the meaning and structure of the language. That means we're distorting phonics by taking it out of the language context.

➤ We're beginning with abstractions instead of functional, meaningful language that's easy to learn.

➤ We're postponing the payoff: the joy of getting the story or the message of the print.

➤ We're ignoring — or even worse, penalizing — learners for dialect differences. In doing so, we're confusing those learners already less likely to succeed in school.

If we support our pupils in developing their phonic generalizations while they're learning to make sense of print, then we avoid these mistakes. In *Through the Looking Glass* Lewis Carroll said it well: "Take care of the sense and the sounds will take care of themselves."

Bibliography

Adams, Marilyn Jager. *Beginning to Read: Thinking and Learning about Print.* Cambridge, MA: MIT Press, 1990.

Adams, Marilyn Jager. *Beginning to Read: Thinking and Learning about Print, a Summary.* Champaign, IL: Center for the Study of Reading, 1990a.

Anderson, R.C., E.H. Hiebert, J.A. Scott, and I.A.G. Wilkinson. *Becoming a Nation of Readers: The Report of the Commission on Reading.* Champaign, IL: Center for the Study of Reading, 1985.

——. Quoted in "Whole language in perspective" by Marilyn Hinds, in *The Reading Reform Foundation Basic Information and Catalog.* Undated, 14-15.

Armstrong, Senator William. "Senate approves Armstrong amendments to improve literacy," in *News from Bill Armstrong, U.S. Senator for Colorado,* February 6, 1990.

Armstrong, Senator William. *Illiteracy: An incurable disease or education malpractice?* Washington, DC: U.S. Senate Republican Committee, September 13, 1989.

Blumenfeld, Samuel L. "Some Houston schools dump whole language and return to phonics (. . . And more on the whole language fraud)," in *The Blumenfeld Education Letter,* 8.2, February, 1992.

——. "The 'Whole Language' Fraud," in *The Blumenfeld Education Letter,* IV.3, March, 1989.

Chall, Jeanne S. "The Case for Teaching Phonics in Schools," syndicated column. Scripps Howard News Service, June 10, 1991.

——. *Learning to Read: The Great Debate.* New York: McGraw-Hill, 1983.

——. "Learning to Read: The Great Debate 20 Years Later — A Response to 'Debunking the Great Phonics Myth'," in *Phi Delta Kappan,* March 1989, 521-538.

——. *Stages of Reading Development.* New York: McGraw Hill, 1983.

——. Quoted in "From a 'Great Debate' to a Full-Scale War: Dispute Over Teaching Reading Heats Up" by Robert Rothman, in *Education Week,* IX.26, March 21, 1990, 10-11.

Chomsky, Noam. *Aspects of the Theory of Syntax.* Cambridge, MA: MIT Press, 1965.

Clay, Marie. *Reading: The Patterning of Complex Behaviour.* Auckland, NZ: Heinemann Educational Books, 1979.

Cronnell, Bruce. "Annotated Spelling-to-Sound Correspondence Rules," in *Tech Report 32*. Los Angeles, CA: Southwest Regional Laboratory, June 1971.

Cummings, D.W. *American English Spelling: An Informal Description*. Baltimore, MD: The John Hopkins University Press, 1988.

Ferreiro, Emilia and Ana Teberosky. *Literacy before Schooling*. Portsmouth, NH: Heinemann Educational Books, 1982.

Fries, Charles. *The Structure of English*. New York, Harcourt, 1952.

Gollasch, Frederick Vincent. "Readers' perception in detecting and processing embedded errors in meaningful text," unpublished doctoral dissertation. Tucson, AZ: University of Arizona, 1980.

Goodman, Kenneth S. "Analysis of Reading Miscues: applied psycholinguistics," in *Reading Research Quarterly*, 5.1, 1969.

———. "Cues and Miscues in Reading: A Linguistic Study," in *Elementary English* 42.6, 1965, 635-642.

———, Editor. *The Psycholinguistic Nature of the Reading Process*. Detroit, MI: Wayne State University Press, 1967a.

———. "Reading: A Psycholinguistic Guessing Game," in *Journal of the Reading Specialist*, May 1967, 126-135.

———. "Unity in Reading," in *Becoming Readers in a Complex Society*. 83rd Yearbook of the National Society for the Study of Education, Part I, Alan C. Purves and Olive Niles, editors. Chicago, IL: University of Chicago Press, 1984, 79-114.

Goodman, Kenneth S. and Carolyn L. Burke. *Theoretically Based Studies of Patterns of Miscues in Oral Reading Performance*. Final Report, Project No. 9-0375. Washington: US Office of Education, April 1973.

Goodman, Kenneth S. and Yetta M. Goodman. "Reading of American Children Whose Language is a Stable Rural Dialect of English or a Language Other Than English." Final Report, Project NIE-C-00-3-0087. Washington, DC: US Department of HEW, National Institute of Education, 1978.

Goodman, Yetta M. "The Development of Initial Literacy," in *Awakening to Literacy*, edited by Hillel Goelman, Antoinette A. Oberg and Frank Smith. Portsmouth, NH: Heinemann Educational Books, 1984, 102-109.

———. "The Roots of Literacy," in *Forty-fourth Yearbook of the Claremont Reading Conference*, Malcolm Douglas, editor. Claremont, CA: Claremont Graduate School, 1980.

———. "A Two-Year Case Study Observing the Development of Third and Fourth Grade Native American Children's Writing Processes." Research funded by the National Institute of Education, Project NIE-G-81-0127, with Sandra Wilde, Lois Bird, Sherry Vaughn, Wendy Kasten and David Weatherill. Tucson, AZ: University of Arizona, 1984a.

Goodman, Yetta M., Dorothy Watson and Carolyn Burke. *Reading Miscue Inventory: Alternative Procedures*. New York: Richard C. Owen, 1987.

Goodman, Yetta M. and Sandra Wilde. *Literacy Events in a Community of Young Writers*. New York: Teachers College Press, 1992.

Groff, Patrick. "Preventing reading failure: The myths of reading instruction," monograph. Washington: US Department of Education, 1987.

Halliday, Michael. "Foreword," in *Breakthrough to Literacy: Teacher Resource Book* by David Mackay et al. London: School Council, 1972.

———. *Learning How to Mean: Explorations in the Development of Language*. London: Edward Arnold, 1975.

Hanna, Paul, J.S. Hanna, R. Hodges, et al. "Phoneme-Grapheme Correspondences as Cues in Spelling Improvement," report. Washington, DC: US Government Printing Office, 1966.

Huey, Edmund B. *The Psychology and Pedagogy of Reading*. New York: Macmillan, 1908.

Iserbyt, Charlotte T. "Reading Is the Civil Rights Issue of the '90s," in *AFA Journal*, March 1990, 17-18.

Johnson, Samuel. *A Dictionary of the English Language*. London: J & P Knapton, 1755.

Kline, Carl L. and Carolyn Lacey Kline. "The Epidemic of Reading Disabilities," in the *Basic Information and Catalog*. Tacoma, WA: Reading Reform Foundation, undated, 6.

Krashen, Stephen. *The Input Hypothesis: Issues and Implications*. London, New York: Longman, 1985.

Labov, William. *Sociolinguistic Patterns*. Philadelphia, PA: University of Pennsylvania Press, 1972.

Lee, Lianju. "Developing Control of Reading and Writing in Chinese," unpublished doctoral dissertation. Tucson, AZ: University of Arizona, 1989.

Miller, George. "The Magic Number Seven Plus or Minus Two: Some Limits on our Capacity in Information Processing," in *Psychological Review* 63, March 1956, 81-92.

Mitchell, Alanna. "Parents Attack the Problem," in *The Globe and Mail*, January 12, 1993.

Nikiforuk, Andrew. "Andrew Nikiforuk on the link between reading difficulties and kids' emotional problems," in *The Globe and Mail*, December 11, 1992.

Osuna, Adelina Arellano. "Oral Reading Miscues of Fourth Grade Venezuelan Children from 5 Dialect Regions," unpublished doctoral dissertation. Tucson, AZ: University of Arizona, 1988.

Piaget, Jean. *Psychology and Epistemology*. New York: Grossman, 1971.

Read, Charles. *Children's Creative Spelling*. London: Routledge & Kegan Paul, 1986.

Smith, Frank. *Understanding Reading*, 3rd edition. New York: Holt, Rinehart and Winston, 1982.

Vygotsky, Lev. *Mind in Society*. Cambridge, MA: Harvard University Press, 1978.

Webster, Noah. *American Dictionary of the English Language*. New York: White & Sheffield, 1828.

———. *Elementary Spelling Book: being an improvement on the American Spelling Book*. Cincinnati, OH: E. Morgan & Co., 1829.

Weir, Ruth and Richard Venezky. "Spelling to Sound Correspondence," in *The Psycholinguistic Nature of the Reading Process*, Kenneth S. Goodman, editor. Detroit, MI: Wayne State University, 1968.

Wilde, Sandra. *You Kan Red This!: Spelling and Punctuation for Whole Language Classrooms, K-6*. Portsmouth, NH: Heinemann, 1992.

Woodley, John Wayne. "Perception of Tachistoscopically Presented Lines of Print," unpublished doctoral dissertation. Tucson, AZ: University of Arizona, 1983.

Index

PLEASE NOTE The following terms appear too frequently to be indexed: alphabet, comprehension, consonants, convention(al), cues, English, inventions, language (oral/written), letter(s), linguists, listening, making meaning/sense, predict(ion), reading/reading process (general), phonics (general meaning), signs, speaking/speech, syllables, symbols, vowels, words, writing/writing process (general).